A 20TH CENTURY APOSTLE

THE LIFE OF ALFRED GARR

A 20th Century Apostle, The Life of Alfred Garr
Copyright © 2003 by Steve Thompson

International Standard Book Number 1-929371-38-1

Distributed by MorningStar Publications, Inc.
A division of MorningStar Fellowship Church
P.O. Box 440, Wilkesboro, NC 28697 USA

MorningStar's Website: www.morningstarministries.org
For information call 1-800-542-0278

Cover Design and Book Layout by Micah Davis
All rights reserved.
Printed in the United States of America.

A 20TH CENTURY APOSTLE

APOSTLE

THE LIFE OF ALFRED GARR

STEVE THOMPSON
ADAM GORDON

DEDICATION

This book is dedicated to my wife Angie and our five children: Jon, Joshua, Madison, Moriah, and Olivia.

You have changed my life by provoking a love within me that I never thought possible. You are living proof that God is gracious to undeserving men such as me.

ACKNOWLEDGEMENTS

Special thanks to Adam Gordon for your persistant dedication to the research required for this project.

Thanks also to Carrie Irvin and Deborah Joyner Johnson for your remarkable skill and grace while editing this project.

TABLE OF CONTENTS

CHAPTER ONE

TOUCHING THE BONES

Some of the best teaching in the Bible does not emerge from the teachings and sermons recorded there. Instead it comes from the stories of simple people who were touched by God. Written instructions and recorded sermons are great and necessary, but seeing how God moved in someone else's life is powerful because it provides instruction *and* encouragement.

Many believers are currently in need of encouragement and revival. Some Christians, who once burned hot and brightly for God, now find themselves lukewarm and dim. Like the church of Sardis they have a reputation for being alive, but are really dead. God can revive them and the stories of past Christian heroes are part of that reviving process.

We find this principle hidden within this strange miracle recorded in II Kings:

> **And Elisha died, and they buried him. Now the bands of the Moabites would invade the land in the spring of the year.**
>
> **And as they were burying a man, behold, they saw a marauding band; and they cast the man into the grave of Elisha. And when the man touched the bones of Elisha he revived and stood up on his feet (II Kings 13:20-21 NAS).**

This is a strange story. Frightened men drop their friend into Elisha's grave. When his dead body touched Elisha's bones, he came back to life. This miracle is awesome, but somewhat capricious at first glance. In reality, this miracle is a powerful prophetic sign showing how the dead can be revived—not just the physically dead, but the spiritually dead.

Bones represent the core values or essence of something. Touching the bones of these past heroes speaks of identifying and being impacted by the core values of their lives. Those who are spiritually weak or dead can be revived by touching the bones of heroes of faith who have walked in spiritual power and authority.

That is the purpose of this book, enabling the reader to touch the bones of Alfred Garr, an ordinary man who lived an extraordinary life. His life is an encouragement to every believer regardless of their current spiritual condition. The account of how he rose from a nominal believer to become an apostle of the twentieth century church is a remarkable and impacting story.

A Spiritual Pioneer

Alfred Garr shook up the world wherever he went. Hundreds of churches throughout the United States and worldwide were birthed through his ministry. He was also a vital, but until now, hidden leader in the Azusa Street Revival. The story of his leadership at Azusa is a powerful lesson for our times.

He also pioneered the healing ministry throughout the United States and helped prophetically steer the course of several Pentecostal movements at strategic moments in their history. A couple of these movements may not have survived without his leadership. He had an uncanny gift for being in the right place at the right time to serve God's purposes.

Alfred Garr was in all ways a true apostle of the twentieth century. And just as with the first century apostles, the *world* took notice of his ministry, not just the church. Consider a few newspaper headlines that reported on his evangelistic campaigns throughout the United States.

Miraculous Cures Are Related By Sufferers At Faith Healing

Garr Meeting Here Attracts Crippled Man Who Throws Away Crutches and Walks; Deaf Woman Says She Hears.

Scenes reminiscent of pictures of Biblical times were re-enacted last night at the tent on West-Trade street where Dr. A. G. Garr, Los Angeles evagenlist, is conducting a revival meeting, as more than a score of cripples and sufferers from various ailments, after having been prayed over by the preacher, testified to miraculous healing.

One elderly man, J. T. Hawkins,

BAKERSFIELD, CALIFORNIA, FRIDAY, SEPTEMBER 8, 1922

Healers Create Stir Here

* * *   * * *   * * *   * * *

Faithful Testify to Cures

Throngs Attend Meetings of Revivalists to See Purported Miracles

Lad Beats Police to Job; Shows Up Before His Arrest

By THELMA BERNARD

AFTER two healing services conducted by R. J. Erickson and A. G.

Diogenes appears to have over-

JT AND THE NORFOLK LANDMARK, THURSDAY, JULY 14, 1927

Prayer-Healing Preacher Hears Others Relate How Faith Cured Their Ills

TOBYHANNA UNITS RETURN FROM 'WAR'

Interest Growing In "Modern Miracles" Testified To In Tent Meeting

Commodore Takes A

Gen. E. S. Fagg, C.
joys the unique privileg
the insignia of a comm
Confederate Navy when
sion demands, went up
terday. He did it litera

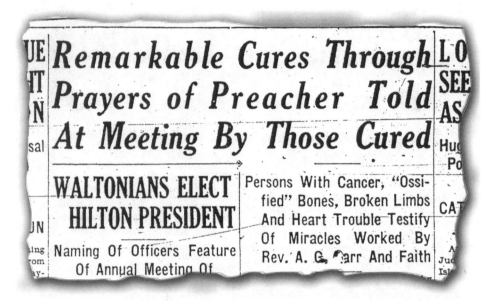

These were not headlines from Alfred Garr's newsletters to his supporters. These were newspaper headlines from major, twentieth century United States newspapers. Additionally, these headlines were often written by those skeptical of the gospel. But the quality of Alfred's ministry was such that it demanded attention, even among unbelievers.

Through a ministry filled with supernatural healings and miracles, Alfred eventually became known as the "man who prays sick people well." In several cities, there were public displays created from the crutches, braces, and wheelchairs abandoned by people healed through his ministry.

Modern Day Apostle

As the western church today grapples with the definition and function of apostles in our modern world, Alfred Garr stands as an encouragement and challenge to our modern concepts of an apostolic life. His life and ministry dramatically illustrate the power and principles underlying true apostolic ministry.

He established churches. Signs and wonders were seen throughout his ministry. He pioneered the gospel throughout the nations. He mobilized and released others into ministry and missions. He provided strategic leadership and help for different parts of the body of Christ in their times of crisis, and sought to build others at his own expense.

He was seldom willing to enjoy the benefits of his success in ministry; he focused instead on pioneering works rather than pastoring them. He repeatedly left to others ministries he had birthed, in order to start again from scratch. As a result he consistently needed and found supernatural help from God both in miracles and miraculous provision.

His Bones Can Be Touched

Although he walked in remarkable spiritual authority and power, Alfred Garr was not an untouchable man. He struggled with the same issues most believers do. If his life had been lived on a pedestal, it may have made a great and interesting story, but would not have the same power to revive us. However, that was not the case.

Alfred Garr was a man most believers today can relate to. He struggled to walk with God consistently throughout his early adult life. He vacillated between having great spiritual hunger and with the difficulty of walking out the Christian life. But he eventually found a pathway to holiness and power with God, and emerged into a ministry fruitful beyond his imagination.

The primary goal of this book is to uncover the bones or core values of Alfred Garr, so that we can touch them and be revived. Alfred Garr's bones have power to resurrect and instruct. The secrets he found to overcoming difficulties and persevering in God are still available to us today, and we need to access them.

A secondary goal of this book is to shed light on the apostolic ministry and its function in our day. Alfred Garr lived an apostolic life in the twentieth century world. The story of his life can help clarify and illuminate the function of an apostolic ministry in the modern church and world.

Alfred Garr's life speaks with force and clarity into our generation. His faith, spiritual hunger, and radical obedience are a profound rebuke to our Laodicean lukewarmness, and an encouragement to us to be zealous and repent. It's a story worth telling and worth learning from.

CHAPTER TWO

FEELING AFTER GOD

The Scriptures are mostly silent on Jesus' childhood and this puzzles many people. They wonder why so little information is provided about His early years. While historians have speculated on the reasons, one practical explanation is that prior to His public ministry, few people realized who He was and what He would be accomplishing. The same is true of many leaders throughout history. Few records from their formative years are maintained, so their early years are mostly hidden from us.

Later, when their biographies are produced, a quandary emerges. Pressure surfaces on the writers to accept anecdotes and third hand recollections instead of hard facts in order to present a more complete story. However, discerning readers recognize spurious statements and skepticism often results. Many readers then question the validity of other claims presented as the narrative progresses and much potential benefit is forfeited.

Presented with the quandary mentioned above, the authors have attempted to avoid it. We decided that a believable, but subdued, chapter presented here is preferable to provoking cynicism that might plague the reader throughout the remainder of this book. Alfred Garr's life speaks with force and clarity to our generation, and is a confrontation of our Laodicean lukewarmness. We will not create skepticism by including stories of questionable origin.

There are many unsubstantiated reports about Alfred's childhood, but little documentation has survived. Many of these stories were engaging, but little could be proven through Alfred's testimony or by other written record. However, within those that have survived, several significant themes emerged and they provide the basis for this chapter.

Alfred Garr (with bicycle) pictured with his mother and family, circa 1889

Parental Influences

Alfred Gaeleton Garr was born in 1874 in Danville, Kentucky. He was the fifth and last child of Oliver Preston Garr and the fourth by Oliver's second wife, Josephine. There was no angelic announcement of his birth—no prophetic sign that heralded the impact he would have in the twentieth century. He was a normal child born into a mostly normal family.

Indeed, Alfred's family was normal enough to provide him stability, but unique enough to engender creativity of thought. He was the youngest child in his family by twelve years. His oldest sister was thirty-six years old at Alfred's birth. She and the other children doted on Alfred as much as his mother, who prized a son of her latter years. Recent studies have indicated that many world leaders are raised by doting mothers, and fathers who are considerably more distant. Valid or not, this was the case with Alfred Garr.

His mother, Josephine, was a creative and caring woman who loved her children above everything. She and Oliver were not distant from one another, but were both fiercely independent. Oliver was intense and driven, mostly for success and especially the appearance of success. He was also quite impulsive as we find from one particular incident prior to Alfred's birth.

In a letter to a relative, Alfred's niece, Ilene Grubbs Utz, provides this snapshot of Oliver and Josephine, and their marriage.

> *Our grandfather was a very ambitious fellow. He wanted to go with a large group of men to the Gold Rush in California. Grandmother objected but he felt he would come back rich as many other men had done.*
>
> *He owned a nice farm near Danville, Kentucky (Boyle County) and had a good living and many servants. Josephine did not want any more riches, but he insisted on going and left her with four children to care for.*
>
> *Josephine told him if he went, she would divorce him, which she did. In those days, divorce was almost unheard of and was a disgrace. The farm was sold and they moved to the small town of Shelby City, Ky, where she taught music and took care of the children.*
>
> *After he had been away a year, Oliver returned a rich man. He stopped on the way home and had some sterling silver spoons made from silver dollars. He had our grandmother's initials, J.S.G. engraved on them.*
>
> *Grandfather was in bad health when he returned and begged Josephine to remarry him, which she did, and took care of him until his death in 1888 at the age of seventy.*

Throughout his life Alfred exhibited the strengths of both his parents. Like his father, Alfred was driven to succeed, partially through a visionary calling, but also through dissatisfaction and a belief that more was better and possible. In fact, from early childhood he demonstrated the same driven personality his father possessed, but for the most part his goals were spiritual, not natural.

His mother's strong independence, allied with the ability to forgive and restore, also deeply influenced Alfred and found expression in his life and ministry. Though she had threatened and then divorced Oliver when he left for California, she agreed to remarry him when he returned and repented. Alfred later exhibited the same ability to allow the past to remain buried and the grace to build on it.

In addition to his parents' personalities, another influence on Alfred's life was the diversity of their economic situations throughout his childhood. Often those who find success experience either poverty or wealth in their childhood. Wealth exposes them to the possibilities of success; poverty provides others with the motivation to achieve it. Alfred was blessed to experience both. His family was relatively wealthy during part of Alfred's childhood and struggled at other times. This diversity arose not only from his parents' short divorce, but also from a loss of family wealth for reasons that remain ambiguous.

Feeling After God

When Alfred was quite young he began exhibiting an unusual spiritual hunger, though his family appeared to not have been religiously inclined. At seven, he came under conviction of sin and began searching for God. He was soon baptized in the local Baptist church, but apparently got washed in the water, not in the Blood.

> *At seven years of age the Spirit of God exerted a powerful influence over my soul in conviction of sin and a judgment to come. Subsequent to this the pressure on my head was such that my mother supposed it to be sickness. About this time I joined the Baptist church, trying to find Jesus and hoping, after Baptism, that peace would come to my troubled heart.*

The pastor who baptized Alfred tried to encourage him that it was "well with his soul" now since he had been baptized. But Alfred knew his soul was still troubled. He continued seeking God, painfully aware that he was still distant from Him.

> *I tried to start serving God by joining the church and being baptized. Somehow I didn't feel any different. After going back to the good preacher I said, "Brother, I've joined the church, was baptized, but I feel just the same. I think you must have baptized me wrong and I would like you to baptize me over." The next time I said, "Now, I am going to make sure. I'm going to think of Jesus hanging on the cross this time." The minister baptized me again, but there was still no difference. I was very much puzzled about it and didn't know which way to turn or what to do. Then I thought it must be some ritualistic compliance that I should embrace and be changed, but somehow I had missed it.*

Alfred expected a real experience with God and was not satisfied when he did not find it. Because of this he soon gained a reputation among his family and friends as a religious freak. When asked why he was so preoccupied with spiritual matters, Alfred reported that he was *"feeling after God."* One of his sisters later wrote to another family member that *"a damned religious fool lives here."*

> *During the next years after that I began to wander around from one meeting to another. They were not very spiritual meetings in those days, just ordinary church gatherings. I would go in the different churches and listen to the service the best I could. Then when they would say, 'If there is anybody who wants to unite with the church, come and receive the right hand of fellowship, I would always go forward. They would ask, "Do you belong to a church?" "Yes, the Baptist." "How long since you joined?" "Oh, just a short time ago." "What's the matter? Did they turn you out?" "Oh no, of course not. Only I want something they don't have." I put myself off on those poor elders, deacons and preachers*

time and time again. They never gave an altar call. After a while I was quite a nuisance and nobody knew what to do with me.

Finally, I went to Charleston, West Virginia, seven hundred miles away for I heard there was a good meeting in a Presbyterian Church. I wanted to speak to the young minister about my condition. So I waited around there until I had a chance to talk to him. I asked him what was the matter with me and he said, "You're out from under the umbrella." That was pretty deep thinking for me so I said, "Oh? Just tell me what the trouble is." "Well, we are all covered over by Christ to keep the wrath of God from us and you have stepped out from under the umbrella. That's all."

Finally after I had hunted for a year or two, perhaps longer, I came home and fell down on my knees in the front room. We never used that room, only when we had company come and they put them in there to sleep. It was in the darkest part of the house and lonely. I always felt sorry for anybody who had to sleep in there. I had my face in the old couch and burst out crying and pleading with God. "Oh, God, I have done everything that I know to do and don't feel any different. There isn't any change and I know that I'm not a Christian yet." I cried there until it seemed my heart broke, but you know after it was over I felt a little bit better. After that I often went away by myself. There was a creek in the woods back of the house and the young squirrels were thick there on the hillside. I'd take the gun and snap off a few for my mother. She liked to stew them. And when I was sure that I'd had enough to warrant my coming again I would lay down in the hog paths because it was so steep in the other places that I couldn't get a footing. I would cry and pray and cry until it seemed at times God was right there but I couldn't get hold of Him. Many times I would go home with my face all dirty and my mother would say to me, "What in the world is the matter with you?" Then I would give her some evasive answer—"Well, it was hot out there and I was sweating." And I was.

Many times I would come home from school and hide away in the little closet praying until my mother began noticing me doing this. She was uneasy. She would say, "Look here, haven't you joined the church?" She didn't know how many times I had joined the church. "Yes, I have joined the church." "You have quit playing 'keeps'?" "Yes, I don't play 'keeps' anymore." "You have stopped telling lies?" "Yes." "Well, isn't that enough? Tell me. Isn't that enough? Why in this wide, wide world do you want to keep on praying like that? Why do you want to go around sniffing in the closets the way you do? What's the matter with you?" "Don't know, but I feel awful good when I go in there and sniff." I meant it too. I did feel ever so much better.

As Alfred continued seeking God, he had a number of powerful encounters. But they only created more hunger. Each time Alfred was touched by God in any way, he was convinced that more was available, but just beyond his reach. His family could not grasp what was happening to him, but Alfred continued to press further in his seeking.

Impact of His Hunger

His friends and family may not have understood Alfred's spiritual hunger, but several were still impacted by it. As his hunger continued and increased, it began bearing fruit among his siblings. A number of them came under conviction of sin and were saved, and so was an early schoolteacher.

I bought a little pocket testament and put it in my desk and would read and mark it whenever I had a chance. Years later my professor came to me and told me with tears in his eyes after I was grown up and heard me preach, "When I found that little testament in your desk, a little testament that was marked and tear stained, my heart hurt me so all the time." (He wasn't a Christian at the time.) "Every time I would think of one of my little pupils carrying a testament around, it got on my nerves. I didn't know what to do." After that, the well-educated and learned man came to the altar and cried out to God and was saved.

I kept talking to the older boys about my experience until finally I got one or two. All of them were afraid of me for they had heard I was going crazy, but when I could get one of them to go to Sunday school with me I was so glad a flood of joy would burst over me and it would seem as though I had a prize with that ragamuffin walking along beside me dirty, barefoot, torn clothes, tossed hair and dirty ears, but just the same I was happy.

Worldly Church Influence

Entering his teen years, Alfred began experiencing the normal struggles of life. At this crucial time, he received little helpful teaching from the churches he attended. In fact, like many believers before him, he grew despondent through the teaching he did receive. His childlike simplicity of seeking God's presence and trusting Him was soon abandoned and he began the sporadic, inconsistent walk of most nominal Christians.

Seeking help in different churches, he found no solution to his dilemma. It only grew deeper. He was plainly told that a more spiritual life, including victory over sin, was unattainable. He was told that sin would always have dominion over him and with this expectation he soon found himself fulfilling this wrong concept. The compromised life was not only preached to him, it was modeled as well.

I knew little about the Word, and being told by preachers and people that I could not live without sin, I soon found myself more deeply in the mire than ever. I then thought I had sinned away my day of grace, because I had put my hand to the plow and had turned back. I turned to the Campbellite Church for relief and was baptized again, but no amount of water can wash sin stains.

I formed the habit of using tobacco. To me it seemed no sin, as the elders and officials did the same. One day I saw a leading man in the church take a glass of whisky. He said, it was for his nerves. With little light and this example I again stumbled into sin. Soon after this I was employed by the Chesapeake and Ohio R.R. Co. and as my associations were not conducive to spirituality, I went into the deepest sin of my life.

This continued for several years. Hoping to begin a new life amid different surroundings, I went to Richmond, Va., but found sin followed me. Having to return to Lexington, Ky., on account of sickness, I faced my mother and sisters with remorse of conscience. After some time I began to read the Bible and the Spirit guided me to the sixth chapter of Hebrews. I saw the doom of those who had once known God and had fallen away.

A pattern was established in Alfred's life that has been repeated in too many lives both before and since. He possessed a profound spiritual hunger, and desired to be holy, but was told it was impossible. Instead of being commended for his hunger and offered instruction in righteousness, he was damned to hopelessness and despair through bad doctrine. In the vulnerable years of adolescence, he yielded to temptation and became "worldly minded."

Years later, Alfred painfully remembered his wasted years. The Scriptures declare, **"It is good for a man to bear the yoke in his youth" (Lamentations 3:27).** Alfred, who was captivated by God in his childhood, could have been a powerful force for God during his youth, but the churches he attended let him down. Alfred never forgot the greatest hindrance of walking with God during this season was the traditional church, which had become lukewarm and worldly.

Introduced to Holiness

During this season, Alfred had an encounter which radically altered his life. While traveling in Kentucky for work, Alfred met a preacher from the Holiness movement who claimed to have been free from sin for more than twenty-three years.

Previous to this I had never heard that a child of God must live free from sin, but shortly after I had the privilege of hearing a Holy Ghost sermon from a sanctified man who declared that God had kept him for twenty-three years. Many scoffed, but I believed, because the glory of God shown in his face.

The conviction from that sermon never left me and for two years I sought God, until one day, while in the oil house at Olive Hill, Ky., the light broke in on my soul. Although joy filled my heart it was not long before I felt the need of something more.

Remembering the words of that holy man, I sought the same Power that had enabled him to live as he did so long. For two weeks I knew what it was really to "hunger and thirst after righteousness," and one night about seven o'clock, while on the engine and in prayer, I felt the power of God strike me in the heart, and then through my entire being.

In spite of Alfred's backslidden condition, his soul remained relatively soft. The years of seeking God had created a tender place in his heart, although he was bound by sinful behavior. While others mocked this Holiness preacher, Alfred believed him. Stunned by this sermon and the concept, Alfred lived under conviction and almost an apocalyptic sense of God's judgment for the next two years. He eventually found deliverance both from the punishment of sin, and its power as well.

Soon after this I felt the call of God to preach the gospel. I resisted. Time after time God marvelously delivered me from being killed, but still I would not yield. By my disobedience I lost God. All this time I was running on the road. One day I was led to a Holiness camp meeting, and there the Lord revealed to my soul I must preach or go to an everlasting hell. I would never make another trip on the railroad.

Alfred had found sanctifying power, but soon discovered that holiness could not be maintained without obedience. By resisting

God's call to the ministry, he lost the sense of God's pleasure and presence. While seeking to appease his conscience, the Lord spoke again to him at a Holiness meeting. After this encounter, Alfred never shrank back from following God. In fact, he hardly ever walked again. Now he started to run.

CHAPTER THREE

A WALK ON THE WILD SIDE

Throughout church history many leaders have appeared from unexpected places. Some have surfaced from the depths of sin and rebellion to provide leadership in the church. Others have emerged from the radical and even fringe movements of their day to the larger body of Christ. The latter would be the case with Alfred Garr.

Alfred had been disappointed and discouraged with the traditional church throughout his search for God. No church leader had understood or encouraged his spiritual hunger until he encountered someone from the Holiness movement. Since he had been profoundly impacted through the Holiness message, he decided to attend Asbury College for his training in ministry.

Located in Wilmore, Kentucky, near Lexington, Asbury was a bastion of the Holiness movement. Such was their reputation for holiness that it was once advertised as being "twenty miles from known sin." Alfred arrived there in the fall of 1898 and began his training.

In an effort to redeem his wasted years, Alfred attacked his studies with passion. However, his academic training came to an abrupt halt when he married Lillian Anderson on March 12, 1899. Alfred and his new bride left Asbury two months later since the school was designed for single students only. His preparation for ministry would have to come through other means.

Alfred and Lillian quickly entered the ministry through ordinations both with the Methodist Church and the International Apostolic Prayer Union, a Holiness group lead by Martin Wells Knapp. Knapp was emerging as the acknowledged leader of the radical faction of the Holiness movement and provided Alfred an entrance into many relationships.

Alfred and Lillian Garr, circa 1904

A Historical Backdrop

To understand the spiritual climate that Alfred lived in, it is important to provide a brief historical backdrop. The Holiness movement, which was life changing for him, had begun as a spiritual renewal within some of the mainline denominations in the middle 1800s.

This movement placed a strong emphasis on the personal aspects of Christianity. Prayer, devotion, hearing God's voice, and especially an experience of personal sanctification were the main tenets. They focused on reclaiming an experiential rather than simply institutional Christianity.

Although the movement was ecumenical and included Presbyterians, Quakers, and others, almost half of those involved were from the Methodist Church. But as the twentieth century dawned, the Methodist Church as a whole turned in a different direction. They attempted to marginalize the influence of this movement within their own church by assigning Holiness preachers to difficult, and out of the way congregations.

As a result, a number of pastors and evangelists left the Methodist Church and established new congregations and ministries. Other Methodist ministers decided to stay in their denomination and attempt to bring change from within. Unfortunately, as is often the case, these two different groups birthed from the same spiritual womb, had difficulty recognizing the validity of each other.

Those who "came out" were often considered rebels by those who stayed within the current church structure. Many of those who stayed in the Methodist Church were considered compromisers by those who had started the new Holiness churches. One particularly interesting group that emerged from the Methodist Church during this season of transition was called the Burning Bush.

The Radical Fringe

The Burning Bush began in 1894 as the Metropolitan Methodist Mission. Edwin Harvey and Duke Farson, along with a number of other young people, founded this group as an evangelistic outreach for Chicago area immigrant neighborhoods with no Methodist Church. Within one year the Mission averaged eight hundred young people each week in their Sunday school program.

They were creative in their approach to evangelism and their presentation of the gospel. They used prizes and entertainment to attract crowds of unbelievers and produced the gospel through dramatic presentations. Their buildings were as non-traditional as their methods, since their primary focus was evangelism. As a result of their success, Harvey and Farson quickly emerged as leaders in the Chicago church scene.

In 1897, the Metropolitan Methodist Mission invited Beverly Carradine, a leader in the Holiness movement, to speak at an annual convention they sponsored for their participants. He delivered a gripping message on personal holiness and hundreds of young people filled the altars seeking sanctification in response. The leaders immediately embraced the Holiness message as their main focus. As a result the Metropolitan Methodist Mission radically shifted their focus over the next few years.

By 1901, they had ended their affiliation with the Methodist Church and changed their name to the Metropolitan Holiness Church Association. But they were commonly known as the Burning Bush. They soon became so radical in their beliefs and practices that they alienated almost every prominent, Holiness minister, including Carradine, who had led them into the movement.

Radical Faith

Many movements led by zealous young people have both good and bad aspects. The Burning Bush was no exception. On the good side, the Burning Bush leaders were creative in their approach to ministry and outrageously confident in God. They believed God could do anything, and were convinced He would do it through them. One example was their "Revival Challenge."

The Burning Bush leaders believed that God would bring revival in response to the radical preaching of His Word. They made a public wager to churches in the Chicago area challenging them to prove a revival could not happen in their congregations. They advertised this throughout the Chicago newspapers offering $1000 to any church willing to take the challenge. The church only had to allow a Burning Bush evangelist to hold two weeks of revival meetings in their congregations as their part of the wager.

This revival challenge created a huge buzz in Chicago. The bookies had created betting lines on different aspects of the challenge. The newspaper columnists discussed this challenge separate from the advertisement taken out by the Burning Bush. This made it a hot source of discussion through the city.

Eventually one Methodist pastor took the Burning Bush up on their offer, but was immediately overruled by his bishop. Hearing of this, the Chicago press ridiculed the bishop publicly in their newspaper for his "lack of faith." The bishop soon recanted. The meetings were quickly scheduled and both sinner and saint watched for the outcome.

A sweeping revival broke out in the church as a result of the meetings. People from all walks of life had a powerful encounter with God. Businessmen, gamblers, bartenders, criminals, drunks, and even Bible school students were all saved during these meetings. Many of them had come because of the publicity generated through the wagers and betting lines. The Burning Bush really was aflame with God's fire.

It was within this radical group of believers that Alfred and Lillian Garr found training and preparation for their ministry that would touch the nations. The lessons they learned and the mistakes they made with this group were more valuable than any degree they could have obtained from Asbury College.

Joining the Fringe

Alfred and Lillian met Edwin Harvey and Duke Farson in late 1901, through their relationship with Martin Wells Knapp. As often happens when those who desire a radical life meet those who are living one, a quick bond developed. Hearing about the exploits of this group, like their revival challenge, the Garrs moved to Chicago within a few weeks to join the Burning Bush movement.

The two main thrusts of the Burning Bush during this season were evangelism and discipleship through church planting, and exposing sin and compromise in the church and her leadership. The latter was done primarily through a magazine they published called, *The Burning Bush*. Alfred was soon involved in both aspects of the ministry.

Alfred was initially drawn to the faith of this group, but their radical commitment was equally as impacting. The Burning Bush and other Holiness groups were comprised of deeply devoted believers who were seeking a return to New Testament Christianity. They embraced whatever spiritual disciplines would help them in their pursuit of purity and power.

They were willing to endure profound hardship to pursue God and serve Him in ministry. The Burning Bush trained their evangelists and workers to expect hardship, and prepared them for seasons of lack and periods of forced fasting.

These people not only believed passionately, they lived sacrificially. We gain insight into their thought processes and practices through an article that was published by Alfred in *The Burning Bush* magazine. This was his report from the field on the Thanksgiving meal God provided while they were ministering.

> *Thanksgiving Day has come and gone and nary a red-snouted turkey showed his face in the Faith home. Truly we are glad of it, because the Lord put a good thanksgiving fast on us and fed us on something better than red-nosed turkey…*
>
> *We arose before daybreak to thank God and continued until late in the evening…In the service God gave us a message from the skies and blessed the congregation with deep conviction.*
>
> *Tests are food to our faith…Sometimes the need was so great that we had to do without food, but we praised God for the lesson. At such times the Lord came so close…*

The Holiness people of the early twentieth century were pioneers. They were seeking deeper encounters with the Lord and were willing to pay the price to live and preach a radical gospel. Their aggressive faith and strong commitment helped Alfred formulate his own personal code of faith and conduct. As opposed to the Campbellite leadership of his youth, these people lived beyond the temporal world.

On the Job Training

The Burning Bush, although influential, was still relatively small numerically when the Garrs joined them. This afforded the Garrs many unique opportunities unavailable in larger, more stable organizations. These opportunities and the experience (and experimenting) they provided to Alfred were especially important.

The Burning Bush's focus was on establishing independent congregations by a systematic approach based on both faith and some promotional principles used in business. According to church historian, Bill Kostlevi, the general pattern of the Burning Bush was set.

> *Schedule a convention in a large public hall and a team of evangelists would be sent to the city who would further publicize the services through a series of noisy open-air street meetings. Exploiting the not infrequent controversies which followed such meetings, the MCA was assured considerable coverage in the local press which invariably resulted in large crowds for their services.*

The Burning Bush leaders had learned the power of publicity during their revival challenge years earlier. They were able to use it to further the kingdom of God. Although they were headed toward some significant mistakes in their movement, the Burning Bush had an awesome vision. They were attempting to recover the power of New Testament Christianity by utilizing twentieth century technology.

The Burning Bush leadership was remarkably progressive in a number of other ways as well. During Alfred's time with the movement, they maintained a policy of not charging for any ministerial services, regardless of the cost to them personally. This included requests for healing prayer which often came from considerable distances.

They were willing to send ministers at no cost across great distances because they were radical, but also because they recognized the training value of these opportunities. Alfred, and later students from their training school, were sent to serve those needing help. One trip was described by Garr in the August 1902 edition of *The Burning Bush*.

> *A lady who has been sick with something like a cancer requested prayer…her son desired someone from the church to go…and pray the prayer of faith. After prayer we decided to make the trip of about four hundred miles by rail, then more by stage…We arrived…after an all night ride…The appearance (of the mother) was, she would bleed to death soon, as the hemorrhages were very distressing…We gathered the family to her bedside and began praying.*

> *Alfred and Lillian led the unsaved family members to the Lord and encouraged them to seek God for sanctification. The woman was not completely healed by the time they left. However, she was sitting up and able to eat and five people had come to the Lord. The family was touched so deeply that the Garrs were invited to return a year later and hold revival meetings on this woman's property.*

Hunger for Supernatural Power

As Alfred tested his theories and ideas in practical ministry settings, he became convinced that divine healing was a key to winning the lost. Divine healing was still a relatively new concept in the church, but Chicago was the center of another movement whose goal was restoring this grace to the church. John Alexander Dowie led this movement.

We gain insight into Alfred's emerging theology from part of an article he published in *The Burning Bush* magazine in the middle of 1902.

> *We find no place in the Word that authorizes us to doubt God's willingness to heal the same as of yore, but we do find abundant*

proof in the Scriptures and experience also that God heals the sick in answer to the prayer of faith.

He goes on to describe healing services at local Salvation Army meetings.

> *I was an eyewitness to a remarkable miracle of healing. While some forty or more were saved...Several cases of healing occurred...one in particular being worthy of special notice. A man suffering from dropsy desired the friends to pray for him that he might be healed. As the "prayer of faith" went up to God the power fell upon him in such a marvelous manner that those kneeling near him felt that the Supernatural was there. He was instantly healed. The swelling in his limbs immediately disappeared and he leaped for joy and praised God...All glory be to Jesus for His healing power.*

Soon the Burning Bush embraced healing not only as a grace available to believers, but as another regulation for holy living. They quickly surmised that faith in God should be enough and began discouraging doctor visits for any reason. These are W.E. Shepard's comments about healing.

> *All sickness and disease comes from the devil and is the result of sin, either directly or indirectly...There are three great works of the devil. Sin in the act; the second is sin as the principle; the third is sickness and death...Divine healing is the quickest method of getting healed...divine healing is the cheapest method. To trust God for physical healing holds one close to Him...Divine healing...uplifts the soul...it exalts Jesus Christ...it is God's method...Folks get converted where people are healed.*

Although we may consider their approach extreme, they had good results. During the time that Alfred was a part of the Burning Bush movement, their success rate in healing the sick was higher than the medical establishments of their day. While the medical profession was not nearly as advanced as it is today, this is still a remarkable statistic.

Even though he helped initiate the Burning Bush's belief in and pursuit of healing power, Alfred was not their most successful "healer." He mostly saw partial healings and symptomatic relief in response to his prayers. Often this came only after days of fasting and prayer for one individual. While he would later become famous for outstanding miracles of healing, these were not seen in the early part of his ministry.

Evangelism and Church Planting

Alfred emerged as a gifted evangelist and church planter during his days with the Burning Bush movement. The Burning Bush and another radical Holiness group, the Pillars of Fire, often held joint campaigns. At one cooperative revival meeting in Kewanee, Illinois, Alfred and Lillian were chosen to disciple and encourage a small band of believers. This became their first pastorate.

Alfred had no experience as a pastor, and was more of an evangelist than teacher, so rather than pastoring by securing the previous advance, Alfred decided he would just keep advancing. Soon these meetings superceded those that had preceded his arrival. So much so that the Burning Bush leadership soon sent additional laborers and began another campaign in the Kewanee area.

While this second campaign was going on, the Holiness ranks in the city contentiously split into two factions. The former leaders of the Holiness movement there began meeting in homes while Alfred continued having upwards of one thousand people attending his meetings.

The division that followed the Burning Bush success in Kewanee underscored the emerging problem in their movement. They were quickly bringing as much division as they were blessing to the church. It would eventually cost them dearly.

An Apostolic Pattern Emerges

The success in Kewanee opened significant doors for Alfred. Soon, he became a featured evangelist for the Burning Bush's jointly held conventions and crusades with another Holiness group, the Pillars of Fire. He resigned from leading the Kewanee congregation in the middle of 1903, so he could focus on evangelism and church planting. This began a pattern which remained through much of Alfred's ministry.

His practice was to come into a city and ignite a spiritual fire through confrontational preaching or through praying for the sick. As new believers gathered and momentum grew, he would then turn over the work to teachers and pastors to disciple the new believers.

From a human perspective he appeared to be a driven or restless man who could not stay in one place for very long. But from a heavenly perspective he was a man who followed God's directive to lay foundations and release others to fulfill their calling.

This is one key attribute of apostolic ministers. Instead of coming to an established work and overseeing it, Alfred initiated or birthed new congregations and left them in others' hands. Like Paul who did not want to build on another man's foundation, Alfred preferred to go to new fields, not existing ones. His mandate and methods were apostolic.

The Good, the Bad, *and* the Ugly

As mentioned previously, the Burning Bush eventually grew extreme in many aspects. They took the teachings of the Holiness movement, which should have been an encouragement of the grace that God had extended to human beings, and fashioned them into a litmus test of "true Christianity."

Now instead of using the local press to stir up interest and crowds to preach the gospel to, they began using their own magazine to attack other Christians. Any minister, denomination, or group who did not live according to their standards of holiness was considered fair game. They began aiming their fire at the church, not the enemy.

They publicly rebuked anyone they felt was compromising the standard of the gospel they preached. Arrogance had emerged in the Burning Bush, and in their own minds they were the only ones living the uncompromised life of holiness and faith. Unfortunately, Alfred distinguished himself in this respect as well. He wrote this in *The Burning Bush*.

> *If ministers would get out of the way, I could hold a successful revival meeting anywhere this side of hell.*

> *Sinner, backslider, cold church member, cooled off Holiness preacher, compromising, money loving, ease seeking professor of Holiness, beware! Hell is waiting for you…*

In another article he attacked the newsletters and ministry reports of other Holiness ministers. He wrote that he and Lillian did not report on their meetings more often because of their disgust in reading reports in other Holiness magazines.

> *For instance, you pick up the Pentecostal Herald…and there you will find a long string of flattery known as, "Reports from the Field." Some read like this:*

> *Brother So and so and wife have just closed a meeting in "Sleepy Hollar," Ky. The fire fell, altars crowed, numbers converted and sanctified, etc. Never has there been such a meeting before in the history of this community.*   *– N.G. Cooled Off Pastor.*

> *Then the evangelist writes a report and flatters the pastor so he can get another call next year, which is somewhat on this order: "The pastor at Sleepy Hollar, called us to help in a revival. He is a lovely man, sweet-spirited, cool-headed and warm-hearted, the right man in the right place. His dear wife is a lovely character. She makes fine biscuits and presides with a queenly grace at the organ…"*

May God help us to preach the Bible truth, leaving the results with God, without flattering some two-headed pastor or evangelist that we may retain his favor.

What had begun as an open, creative, evangelistic mission quickly evolved into a strange consortium of spiritual values. On one hand, they were a strongly evangelistic, church planting, faith ministry. On the other hand, they became a divisive, legalistic sect that used their print pulpit to assassinate the character of prominent ministers and large segments of the body of Christ.

However, they were still filled with creativity in the midst of their emerging control spirit. Every member of their movement was expected to play an instrument and actively participate in leading worship. They were called "holy jumpers" by most of their detractors because their worship was so exuberant it unnerved them. But it was not just loud, it was creative and musically excellent.

A More Poisoned Pen

Soon any behavior that the Burning Bush considered not in accordance with the sanctified life was the target of their poison pen. In early 1904, Alfred wrote a criticism of the Salvation Army.

The Salvation Army backslid because they lost faith in God's power to provide for their temporal needs and now we behold them begging pennies on the street corners.

Two years earlier Alfred had praised the Salvation Army for the power of God in their meetings. He had reported on healings and the salvations that he witnessed. But Alfred, like the other Burning Bush leaders, had become arrogant and condemning toward other Christian leaders and movements.

With his reputation as a hardnosed preacher and confrontational expert, Garr soon became the Burning Bush's primary hatchet man. He began investigating the supposed improprieties of other

41

ministers and their doctrinal leanings, and reported on them in *The Burning Bush* magazine.

Quickly, the articles degenerated from examining theological differences and supposed improprieties to mocking the personalities. One example is his report on Charles Weigele, a minister who had held meetings in the same city as Alfred. Weigele had kissed an unmarried woman on the cheek and this was considered scandalous by the Holiness movement.

> *Charles Weigle is in town but not in the Spirit. Came here for 10 days of meeting and closed in 6 days. Meeting fizzled and closed last night.*

> *The Rev. Seventy five Dollar, Charlie Kissing, Cooing, Weigele closed a gigantic failure called a revival in Danville, Va., a few days ago. He informed the people that he was not fighting the devil; that the Spirit of God was the dove-spirit, and did not fight but cooed…The first trip he kissed, the second he cooed.*

> *Charlie has so completely cooled off that even the Rev. Dr. Troast, pastor of the Methodist Episcopal, Baptist Campbelliteish conglomeration of ecclesiastical sticks, endorses him…he left the hypocrites, backsliders and sinners more hardened for hell.*

The Burning Bush, though blessed of God, was cutting short their influence on the earth, by dishonoring their spiritual fathers and mothers. Unfortunately, Alfred was right in the thick of things. In spite of this caustic attitude, they remained successful in their evangelistic endeavors. They had a sincere desire to see the lost saved; unfortunately they believed almost everyone was lost.

Their First Church Plant

Danville, Virginia, represented another milestone in the Garr's development and ministry. In early 1904, Alfred and Lillian began a work in Danville, Virginia from scratch, intending to only stay a few weeks as an evangelist, but something else transpired. Shepard wrote of Garr's success there in their magazine.

> *They (Garrs) opened there in a small way and God began to pour His blessing upon them...God put it on them to take no collections and to not say a word about money. The preaching was very hot and the people had hard work to stand it.*
>
> *The burden for the work there came on them very heavily and they saw that the only thing was to stay right there, so they sent home (Chicago) for workers and we sent them three missionaries. Soon they rented a house and started a Missionary Home, all living together, and expected to take in any needy cases...They are trusting God for provisions and for the furnishings of the house...*

Alfred and Lillian moved to Danville to lead that congregation and it was their home base for the next eighteen months. Alfred wrote about the nature of the work in their first months in dealing with unbelievers and those who were already in churches.

> *The work now, is chiefly, to show them that they are not converted. The preacher who plowed this field, must have had his oxen hitched to a garden rake.*

Danville had been the sight of considerable success for the Holiness movement previously, but not according to Burning Bush standards. Alfred and Lillian believed that the Holiness churches in the area were after money more than souls. They accused these churches of compromising on divorce and remarriage, and caving in on other Holiness standards for financial gain.

The Flames Grow Apart

Although he was now leading the Danville congregation, Alfred continued traveling as a featured evangelist in the joint Burning Bush and Pillars of Fire crusades and conventions. The Garrs and Alma White, leader of the Pillars of Fire, traveled together extensively during the summer of 1904.

It was during this trip that Alfred began to express some disenchantment with the Burning Bush. Alfred apparently confided to Alma White some doubts he had about the integrity of other Burning Bush leaders, primarily because of the addition of a new member to their leadership team. He also began to recognize the control spirit that had infected their teachings and practice.

The Burning Bush now taught that every believer was called to the ministry, either in missions or at home. Though a good concept in itself, they soon made it another requirement for holy living. If a church did not require their people to be involved in ministry, they were considered compromisers and the people, backsliders. They also began enacting greater control over individuals in more aspects of their personal lives.

According to Bill Kostlevi, *"The MCA was no longer content with urging Christians to organize independent congregations. Faithful Christians, following the apostolic precedents established in Acts 2, were urged to sell their possessions and join the rest of God's people at Fountain Spring House."*

Alma White also recognized this control problem and began to distance herself and her group from the Burning Bush. Soon Alfred was the only Burning Bush evangelist that she would talk with. Eventually, these two groups ended their cooperation because of a dispute over ownership of a property in New Jersey. In reality, the Garrs' days with Burning Bush were numbered as well.

A Change in the Air

Over the next year as the Burning Bush continued spiraling toward more controlling doctrine and behavior, Alfred struggled to maintain his zeal for the movement. He was still functioning in some of the same control himself, but was still questioning the direction the movement was headed.

Indeed, a change was coming which Alfred could have never predicted. It would radically and irrevocable alter Alfred's walk and ministry. However, before outlining that episode, it is important to recognize the positive influence the Burning Bush movement had on Alfred and Lillian Garr.

The Burning Bush provided Alfred with spiritual role models who were vital for him. As a young man, Alfred had no good experience with spiritual leaders. In the Burning Bush he found his spiritual mentors. The hard preaching, sacrificial lifestyle, and consistent conduct of Shepard, Harvey, and Farson gave Alfred those he could emulate.

Alfred was not called to do ministry in the traditional way, so being included in a leadership team of a radical, non-traditional ministry was a profound education. Because of the team aspects of the Burning Bush leadership, Alfred was also allowed to observe and participate in the leadership's decision-making process first hand.

Because the Burning Bush was pioneering different works, Alfred and Lillian gained crucial insight into church planting and beginning works from scratch which would prove invaluable later. They also learned to live a life of radical faith and sacrificial service. They learned to enjoy hardship and testing, rather than just endure it.

Overall, they had an experience of God so profound that they were ruined for normal life or for traditional Christianity to satisfy them. Like most believers, Alfred had many opinions and ideas. But when placed in the position of starting works from scratch, the only ideas that survive are the ones that work. Strangely, it was in the Burning Bush movement that became increasingly idealistically driven where Alfred Garr learned practical decision making in ministry.

God was preparing the Garrs to scatter the seeds of a revival movement that would reach the ends of the earth. For all their missionary zeal and radical commitment, and walking on the wild side of radical Christianity, they could never imagine what awaited them next.

In January 1906, the Burning Bush leaders in Waukesha asked the Garrs to leave the Danville congregation and relocate across the country to Los Angeles. The Garrs were conflicted about this request. The Danville work was uniquely their own—plus Alfred was struggling with the current direction of the Burning Bush. The Garrs had an important decision to make, but they could never envision what hinged on their decision.

CHAPTER FOUR

A DATE WITH DESTINY

Alfred and Lillian arrived in Los Angeles during February 1906, the same month as William J. Seymour, the future leader of the Azusa Street Mission. Seymour was an unknown independent minister; Garr was a national leader of the Burning Bush movement. They had come to Los Angeles for vastly different reasons, but within months God would join them together in an unusual way to radically impact and alter Christianity.

Both Seymour and Garr had become enamored with the teachings of the Holiness movement and each possessed remarkable spiritual hunger. Alfred's lifelong spiritual hunger has been documented in preceding chapters, but William Seymour's heart burned brighter for God than possibly anyone of his day.

Hungry for God

God had begun a significant process of cultivating spiritual hunger in William Seymour's life. For several years, he had fasted weekly and prayed several hours a day for a greater experience in God. After eighteen months of seeking in this manner, the Lord had spoken to him, *"There are greater and better things to be had in the Christian life, but they only come by prayer and fasting."* Seymour had two potential responses to the Lord's instruction—frustration or obedience.

He had already been fasting weekly and praying almost five hours daily for over a year. Most of us today would be exasperated with the Lord for requiring anything above what we already were doing. But Seymour had a fear of God and a love for Him that produced a remarkable humility. He continued his fasting schedule and increased his prayer time from five and a half to seven hours a day.

Seymour's spiritual hunger outstripped all natural, human desires. As an African American, he had endured profound racism, but never allowed it to deter his quest for God. He had earlier "attended" Charles Parham's Bible School in Houston, Texas, but not as a student. He was not allowed to sit in the same classroom as the white students because Parham did not believe in "race mixing."

Instead of reacting, he overcame. He sat in the hallway and listened to Parham teach about the Holy Spirit through the classroom door which was left ajar. William Seymour was so hungry for God that he could gain something of spiritual significance from anyone regardless of their problems or prejudices. His reputation mattered little to him—finding something more in God was his goal.

Seymour arrived in Los Angeles in February 1906, and began holding "prayer and seeking" meetings at a home on Bonnie Brae Street. The resulting Pentecostal revival that emerged from the outpouring at Azusa Street is well known. Indeed, history would be altered by the events which followed, but not without the help of another man who arrived in Los Angeles for completely different reasons.

Putting Out a Fire

As mentioned in the previous chapter, by the middle of 1905, Alfred Garr was established as one of four main leaders of the Burning Bush movement. Because of his success in evangelism and church planting, Alfred had emerged as the "fair haired son" of the movement. He also enjoyed a wider voice into the Holiness movement through his role as an editor of their flagship publication.

In late 1905, Alfred was leading the Burning Bush congregation he had planted in Danville, Virginia, the previous year. Although he continued speaking at conventions and providing leadership throughout the Burning Bush movement, he and Lillian had put down roots in Danville. They had even named their first child Virginia.

Alfred and Lillian with daughter, Virginia, circa 1905

In January 1906, Harvey and Farson asked the Garrs to relocate across the country to Los Angeles. Significant problems had emerged with the Burning Bush congregation there and they asked Alfred to troubleshoot for them. Currently, his former mentor W.E. Shepard was struggling to maintain, much less build, the Burning Bush church in Los Angeles.

The trouble in Los Angeles had erupted when Alma White, their former associate, began to persecute their movement. She had come to Los Angeles to establish a congregation affiliated with her group, the Pillars of Fire. Upon her arrival in Los Angeles in January, she had published an exposé, branding the Burning Bush movement as a controlling cult. This caught the Burning Bush leaders off guard. Within a matter of days, almost 20 percent of Shepard's congregation, many of them leaders, left and joined the Pillars of Fire group.

Harvey and Farson were concerned that Alma White would further damage their work unless decisive leadership was demonstrated and Shepard had not done that. They "requested" that Alfred and Lillian move to Los Angeles and deal with the damage. The Garrs agonized over this request, torn between their love for the Danville congregation and submitting to their leaders. We catch a glimpse of their theology and philosophy of ministry during this time as well.

The devil gets many well meaning people out of the order of the Lord and out of the Spirit by giving them impressions. He will suggest to them that they ought to be in some other town or city or country and that they could have victory some place else, and if the church will not send them they go down in the dumps or else send themselves, and God is not pleased with them...

Alfred continued this article by using military analogies to describe the importance of obeying headquarters, even if you disagree with their directions. He believed that the war as a whole demanded following the orders of spiritual authorities, and trusting that they were getting their information from God. His bottom line sentiment was, "If you don't go, you're a deserter."

God will put orders on headquarters and when you get your orders ask God to give you the victory through the orders that you have from headquarters, and if the orders you have from headquarters are not right get a brand new headquarters that has sense...

Alfred did not believe in blind obedience as is evidenced by the last sentence above. He believed if you could not follow the directions of your headquarters, then you needed to leave that particular movement. He believed in obeying authority, but also recognized that believers had a choice of which authorities to be joined with. He continued:

I will go where I am sent, wherever that is, and I feel I am not called to California or to Illinois particularly; I feel called to the world and wherever I am, I am going to get it (the Lord's burden) on me, and if I go to a place I will get that place on me, and will fast and pray until the burden comes.

Although they received no specific direction toward taking the assignment, they ultimately decided to submit to the wishes of their leaders. Without realizing it, the Garrs had made a choice which would radically alter their lives, and the history of the church in the twentieth century and beyond.

The City of Angels

The Garrs were not strangers to Los Angeles. They had conducted two highly successful revival campaigns there; the last only a few months earlier, near the end of 1905. But upon their arrival, they found the church considerably different than when they left. Now it consisted of only a couple hundred people, with much of the core leadership gone. Currently, the only flames at the Burning Bush congregation were the accusation and slander fanned by Alma White.

Alfred's first action as the west coast director of the Burning Bush movement was to secure new meeting facilities, but not what anyone expected. Instead of downsizing their facility for the current crowd, he obtained a newer, larger facility seating one thousand people. A leader, not an administrator, he had not moved across the United States to manage a shrinking congregation, but to rebuild a bigger and better one.

His second act was to dismiss his former mentor, W.E. Shepard, and assume the pastorate of the church. After a few weeks in Los Angeles, Alfred felt that Shepard had not only lost control of the congregation, but his family as well. Shepard's wife was causing significant trouble in the congregation. Whether it was a reaction to the growing "control spirit" in the leadership at Chicago, or simply her own spiritual problems, she had soon replaced Alma White as the biggest critic of the Burning Bush in Los Angeles.

The main disagreement emerged from the Shepard's decision to enroll their daughter in a local Methodist Christian School. The Burning Bush leaders, Alfred included, denounced this decision as inconsistent with the Burning Bush philosophy. How could a pastor who taught the higher truths of the Holiness message, largely rejected by the Methodist Church, allow his child to have her mind shaped by backsliders and compromisers?

Alfred confronted Shepard for failing to control his wife and when they could not agree, Alfred excommunicated his former mentor from the congregation. We gain insight into Alfred's thought processes and the inner workings of the Burning Bush movement through a letter Alfred sent to headquarters.

April 25, 1906

Dear Brothers Harvey and Farson:

Who shall be able to stand...I do not think it is consistency to preach against the Free Methodists as an institution, and then patronize them as an institution (daughter went to their school)... I could hardly sleep it troubled me so much. Finally I went to Shepard in regard to the matter and he said he would pray about it.

I have visited Sister Shepard several times and nothing but stings and virus for the folks in Waukesha and especially you two brethren. I told Brother Shepard he would have to restrain her and I told him all my heart, i.e., that I believed she was filled with the devil and was his and our worst enemy. He said he did not believe she was full of the devil. I told him that I thought best for him to resign if he were going to send Merle to that school.

The Lord showed me this afternoon that he is not going through and that he listened to the slime of his wife until God is grieved...I am sorry that God had to cut him off, but I think it is for the best. May God have mercy on him.

Just before I received his resignation, God showed me clearly that He would not bless us while he was here unless he restrained his wicked wife and pulled Merle out of that school.

This afternoon I received his resignation, which I enclose. Please save it. We have no differences between us of a bitter nature in the least, but he came to the place where he had to decide between his wife's will and God's will. And then I was placed in a similar position to decide between God, and Brother Shepard, my good friend.

I am broken hearted because I am sure his wife has succeeded in effecting his damnation at last, and she is very happy woman now that he is no more with us. If I ever saw a perfect devil I believe she is one.

One product of the division in the Holiness movement was that it continued to produce other divisions. By forgetting that their battle was not against flesh and blood, many groups were warring more against each other and themselves than the true enemy. The Burning Bush was not only divisive, they ostracized anyone who did not agree with them, and often publicized the process.

Harvey and Farson published the above letter from Garr in *The Burning Bush* magazine for public consumption. Although Alfred had used a poisoned pen to assail others for compromising the gospel, or Holiness message, he had written this letter as a personal field report and never intended it for public consumption.

The Burning Bush had become so controlling and caustic that they were willing to ruin other's reputations in order to protect their own. Their requirement of strict compliance and a scorched earth method of church discipline left little neutral ground for or about them. In many ways, the Burning Bush leadership was proving Alma White's accusations true.

With Alfred clearly in command of the congregation, he now sought to build it through evangelistic campaigns and revival meetings. Even though he had dealt swiftly and harshly with Shepard and his wife, the congregation soon began responding to Alfred's leadership and the accusations ceased.

Soon a good number of visitors began attending the evangelistic campaigns at the new facility and some were converted. Attendance at the congregation increased and the church not only stabilized but grew. The trouble started by Alma White was being dealt with, but the Garrs realized the meetings lacked the intensity of their previous campaigns. In reality the fire of God had already fallen nearby in a very different setting.

The Azusa Street Mission

While the Garrs labored to build through evangelistic meetings, and a larger facility, a small group of saints led by Seymour were taking a different approach. Instead of attempting to attract people, Seymour tried to attract the Lord. His humble gathering focused on prayer, seeking the Lord, and tarrying for the Holy Spirit. They met in a small home and did not advertise their meetings.

The basic meeting format, or one that emerged, consisted of Seymour instructing the people that there were deeper things in God to be found and that prayer and fasting were the pathways. He also taught that God would baptize sanctified believers in the Holy Spirit. The people would then pray and seek God well into the night. Soon God answered their call and began visiting them in a remarkable way. A number of individuals were baptized in the Holy Spirit and spoke in other tongues.

Seymour soon moved the meetings to an old livery stable nearby and named it the Azusa Street Mission. This building was less than two miles from the new facility, which housed the Burning Bush congregation, pastored by Alfred Garr. Although the people were coming to Alfred Garr's meetings, the Lord had decided to attend Seymour's because He had been invited.

The World Takes Notice ... Briefly

Though the Azusa Street Mission was small in numbers, *The Los Angeles Times* sent a staff writer to report on their meetings due to their bizarre nature. When the reporter was present, there were less than two dozen people in attendance. On April 16, 1906, *The Los Angeles Times* ran the following headline on the front page:

Los Angeles Times

WEIRD BABEL OF TONGUES:
New Sect of Fanatics Is Breaking Loose / Wild Scene Last Night on Azusa Street

Colored people and a sprinkling of whites compose the congregation and night is made hideous in the neighborhood by the howlings of the worshipers, who spend hours swaying back and forth in a nerve racking attitude of prayer and supplication. They claim to have the gift of tongues and to be able to comprehend the babble.

Such a startling claim has never yet been made by any company of fanatics even in Los Angeles, the home of almost numberless creeds...

The day this article appeared, a massive earthquake struck San Francisco, devastating the city. Pastors and church leaders immediately pronounced the earthquake as God's judgment upon a wicked society. Larger crowds immediately began attending the Mission. However, this lasted only a few weeks. Soon the crowd had diminished to around a couple dozen believers once again. God was pouring out His Spirit, but very few people were being filled, because very few were attending.

Many people wrongly assume that when revivals occur crowds mobilize immediately. However, from historical accounts we discover the opposite is generally true and was definitely the case at Azusa Street. Although God poured out the Holy Spirit in Los Angeles in early April, historians attest to the small numbers attending until the beginning of the summer months.

Robert Anderson, writes in *Vision of the Disinherited*, *"The work seems to have moved by fits and starts until late summer."* Rachel Sizelove agreed and wrote about her visit in early June: *"There were about twelve of God's children, white and colored, tarrying before the Lord...."* Frank Bartleman, noted historian and revivalist, wrote, *"The 'Ark of God' moved off slowly at 'Azusa' ... a small beginning, a very little flame."*

The Azusa Street *Mission* had been birthed, but the Azusa Street *Revival* had not. God was moving, but the impact was limited to a few individuals and was not progressing in any tangible, numerical way. However, the historical accounts began to report something different occurring after June. In July 1906, Frank Bartleman now wrote that, *"Pentecost has come to Los Angeles."*

Something transpired near the middle of June, which propelled the Azusa Street Mission from a dozen saints seeking the Lord to a revival movement with worldwide impact. What seemingly had more power to draw crowds than a *Los Angeles Times* article or an earthquake reported to be God's judgment? The answer lies in the story of how Alfred Garr abandoned his own ministry ambitions in order to find more of God.

Disenchanted with Success

Alfred and Lillian Garr became increasingly disenchanted in their roles as pastors of the Burning Bush in Los Angeles. They were experiencing success in reawakening the congregation, but they were hungry for something deeper than success. Alfred realized that something was askew in his heart, because his soul was unsatisfied.

For most of his life, Alfred had hungered for God. Even after finding Him and entering the ministry, he continually longed for more. When he and Lillian were asked to relocate to Los Angeles, he submitted to his authorities for the good of the Burning Bush movement. But he had been having misgivings about the Burning Bush for some time already and when Harvey and Farson published his letter about Shepard, it caught Alfred's attention.

It is all too easy to see the wrong in another person or movement, but quite difficult to recognize it within ourselves. This is why Jesus encourages us to deal with the "beam in our own eye, before attempting the removal of the speck in another's" (see Matthew 7:3). When Alfred saw his own words about Shepard and his wife, published in

The Burning Bush magazine, he began to recognize that something was not right in his own soul as well.

As he processed these stirrings, Alfred received reports of a spiritual fire falling at the Azusa Street Mission. He was amazed that God was moving profoundly only two miles away from his own facility. Why had God come to another group, when he was laboring away preaching and holding the church accountable to the Holiness message. He decided to investigate for himself. *Note: Since God's moving at the Azusa Street Mission has been the subject of much writing, it will not be rehearsed here except minimally.*

A New Direction

Alfred began visiting the Mission and was struck by what he discovered. Seeing William Seymour humbly but fervently pour out his heart to God, with his head stuck underneath the pulpit, Alfred's heart was ignited. Alfred recognized that his own spiritual hunger had waned as he had grown into an enforcer instead of seeker of holiness.

In Seymour he found both a kindred spirit and a challenge. He could sense that Seymour's entire life was built around obtaining something more in God. Alfred remembered his years of seeking God and immediately restructured his approach to life and ministry in order to find his own latent spiritual hunger which had ebbed.

He began spending as much time seeking the Holy Spirit, as he did rebuilding the Burning Bush congregation, possibly more. His days centered on tarrying for the Holy Spirit, either at Azusa or at the Burning Bush facility. He did not abandon his pastoral responsibilities; he just realized his need for something more in God and pursued it. He realized that although God was blessing his meetings, they lacked the fire he had experienced at the Azusa Street Mission. Alfred wanted God and he wanted the fire.

One evening in early June, the congregation of the Burning Bush arrived for their regular meeting and found Alfred standing on the front steps, with the church doors locked. He proclaimed, *"Do not attend here tonight. We do not have the power of God; let us go to the Azusa Street Mission, where they are enjoying the presence of God."* Alfred began walking to the Azusa Street Mission and the people followed him.

A Severe Test

The national leadership at the Burning Bush headquarters was less than enthusiastic with Alfred's decision to shut down church meetings and take the congregants elsewhere. They had sent Alfred to Los Angeles to stop the flow of Burning Bush members leaving the congregation and now he was the one taking them other places. Their solution had become part of the problem. But Alfred had questions about his leadership from a closer source.

Lillian soon became convinced that Alfred was deceived and un-balanced. It appeared the suspicion and control which enveloped the Burning Bush was so pervasive that Lillian threatened to leave Alfred if he continued at the Azusa Street Mission. Alfred, after having judged Shepard so harshly about controlling his wife, was now having trouble with his own.

Lillian had actually packed her bags to leave, but Alfred persuaded her to attend the Azusa Street Mission before she left. When they arrived at the Mission that evening, Alfred and Lillian settled near the back of the meeting facility. Lillian's turmoil subsided as she settled into the makeshift pews because the atmosphere of the meeting was very similar to the Holiness circles they had traveled in for years.

Having judged without seeing firsthand, Lillian began backing off of her assumptions and suspicions. Soon after the meeting began, and before she could object, the Lord descended upon Lillian and baptized her in the Holy Spirit, complete with speaking in tongues. Needless to say, Lillian stayed with Alfred.

Deep Dealings

While pursuing the Lord at Azusa, Alfred had seen many people baptized in the Holy Spirit while his tarrying went unanswered. Now, his wife was baptized in the Holy Spirit, without even seeking it. Thankful for her encounter, but more hungry than ever, he sought God more passionately, but found conviction instead of the requested blessing.

As Alfred sought God for the Holy Spirit baptism, the Lord dealt deeply with his fundamental heart issues. The first item was Alfred's pride and his criticism of other ministers, especially his former mentor, W.E. Shepard. God showed Alfred the pain that he caused Shepard through his scathing denunciation of Shepard and his wife to the Burning Bush leadership.

Although Alfred had never meant for his letter to Harvey and Farson to be made public, he was responsible, because those were his words. God revealed the depths of his arrogance in criticizing Shepard and the fact that he had effectively ruined their reputations publicly through his letter to Harvey and Farson. The Lord told him that until he and Shepard were reconciled, he would not baptize Alfred in the Holy Spirit.

Alfred immediately traveled by bicycle to Shepard's home and requested a meeting with him. He apologized, begged for forgiveness, and repented of his wrong attitude and actions. He returned to the Mission, but the Lord immediately sent him back to Shepard. Again, he repented of his attitude and sin, and again Shepard forgave him. But still he found no peace with the Lord.

God would not answer Alfred's request for power until he responded to the Lord's call for purity. As he continued seeking

God, Alfred heard the Lord speak into his spirit, "You do not really love that brother." Alfred cried, "Lord, I will go back and ask him to forgive me again."

He traveled back again to Shepard's home, but this time there was brokenness. As he started up the walkway, Shepherd saw him and began to smile. Alfred placed his arms around his former mentor's shoulders and began to cry. He sobbed, "Please forgive me for the fuss that we had." Shepard began to weep also and said, "I want you to forgive me, too, for I did not act like a Christian."

Alfred traveled directly back to the Burning Bush facility feeling great. As he sought the Lord and waited for the Holy Spirit, he knew he had been cleansed. God spoke to him that he would soon receive the promise. But more conviction was waiting.

The Bottom Line

The Lord began dealing with Alfred's desire for prominence. He confronted Alfred on his need to be seen and admired by others. God asked Alfred if he would be willing to pull a coal wagon, if that was His will. God was putting the axe to the root of Alfred's life, and preparing him for true apostolic leadership, which entailed self-sacrifice and profound humility.

Alfred had considered the ministry a privilege and had chosen to follow God against the wishes of his family. Several of his extended family members were doctors and lawyers, and Alfred had disappointed most of them by pursuing the ministry. Now God was asking if he could humble himself even lower and potentially become a manual laborer.

Alfred was humble enough to encourage his congregation toward the Azusa Street Mission, but could he abandon the prominence of leading a church? Also, it is possible that Alfred had taken over the leadership of the Los Angeles congregation from selfish ambition. This could have been partly responsible for his dismissal of Shepard as well. Regardless of the full measure of the Lord's dealings, Alfred was confronted with a profound test.

Alfred dealt honestly with the Lord until he was confident he could follow, and not just lead. He finally broke through and found that he could honestly walk away from the ministry if the Lord asked him to. As soon as this issue was settled, Alfred Garr was baptized in the Holy Spirit in the bell tower of the Burning Bush facility. It was June 16, 1906.

The Mission Becomes a Revival

Alfred Garr was now ready to prosper. He had now received apostolic power from God and the apostolic gift of speaking in other tongues. However, several days later God spoke to him again. He communicated to Alfred that the recent dealings were not hypothetical in nature.

The question about walking away from leadership was not just a heart issue. God actually wanted him to resign as pastor of the Burning Bush congregation, but not in order to reinstate Shepard. God wanted Alfred to merge the Burning Bush congregation with the fledgling Asuza Street Mission and for Alfred to support William J. Seymour's leadership without asking for any position for himself.

Without any hesitation that we can find, Alfred Garr, the West Coast director of the Burning Bush Movement, shut down the church he was sent to save and merged it with the fledgling Azusa Street Mission. Several hundred people, along with he and Lillian, joined Seymour and his congregation at Azusa Street. As a reward for following God, Alfred's name immediately disappeared from *The Burning Bush* magazine editor's list.

The Mission Becomes a Revival

With this infusion of people and Garr's support of Seymour, the Azusa Street Mission began to blossom. New life was breathed into the meetings as the crowds swelled. When the two congregations merged, a synergy was created, especially as the larger congregation came in humility and joined the smaller one. The fire that had been simmering began to grow and spread as scores and hundreds were baptized in the Holy Spirit.

The Azusa Street meetings turned into a revival when Alfred Garr humbled himself and began supporting a man more anointed than himself. Frank Bartleman, a participant at Azusa testified of the dramatic change which coincided with Garr joining the Mission. In April he had written that it was *"a small flame."* In July, Bartleman reported to the *Way of Faith* magazine: *"Pentecost has come to Los Angeles."* Using a different analogy, the stream had now become a river.

A river is formed as individual tributaries come together, contributing their smaller streams to make a larger body of water. William Seymour was the man God used to initiate the Pentecostal Revival, but he needed assistance. When Alfred Garr, at the expense of his own reputation, obeyed God in humility, and submitted himself to Seymour, the results were phenomenal.

The River Flows

God honors faith. It required faith for Alfred to place his congregation in Seymour's hand. But soon God asked Alfred to take another, more profound step of faith. Believing that he had received not just apostolic power for winning the lost, but also "apostolic languages" to preach the gospel in other nations, Alfred felt called to the nations. Within three weeks after being baptized in the Holy Spirit, Alfred announced in a meeting that God had called him to take the Pentecostal outpouring to India and China.

Seymour immediately halted the meeting and received an offering for the Garrs and another missionary. An offering of $7,000 was received from the members of the mission. The Garrs and the other gentleman were prayed over and sent out of the Azusa Street Mission into the mission field. Alfred Garr had received his commission from God as he abandoned the one given by the Burning Bush Movement.

Stepping Out

Within days, he and Lillian were busy tying up loose ends in order to move toward their mission. They allowed a couple who had been involved with their Burning Bush congregation to live on the church property to be caretakers for the headquarters in Chicago. They packed their belongings and were gone from Los Angeles in days. God had spoken to them and they were obeying.

William J. Seymour was one of the great heroes of the faith in the twentieth century. His hunger for God and refusal to be deterred from his quest are legendary. Without his obedience, the Pentecostal revival would have never begun. But without the obedience of Alfred Garr, it may never have reached its apex in Los Angeles, and it may never have spread very far.

Both of these men embodied the heart of the Azusa Street revival, but their callings were drastically different. If William Seymour was the face of the Azusa Street revival, Alfred Garr was its feet. And the feet were ready to begin carrying the Pentecostal message to the rest of the world.

CHAPTER FIVE

OUT OF THE FOLD

It would be nearly impossible to overestimate the faith which gripped Alfred and Lillian as they traveled across the United States. They believed they had received apostolic power at Azusa Street, and apostolic languages to preach the gospel in India and the Orient. They burned with Pentecostal fire and were prepared to ignite whatever they touched.

Charles Parham, whose Bible school Seymour had tried to attend, taught that the tongues given as evidence of the Holy Spirit baptism were apostolic languages for missionary purposes. He taught that God was gifting them, just as He had the believers in Acts 2, who had been empowered to speak in the languages of the dispersed Jews (see Acts 2:4-11).

When Alfred had been baptized in the Holy Spirit, someone reported that he had been speaking in a conglomeration of Indian dialects including Bengali. Lillian had been understood to be speaking in a Chinese language. As such they determined God had prepared them and was sending them to India and the Orient. The initial Pentecostals believed that God was giving both apostolic power to win the lost, and languages for preaching to them.

Before launching their mission to the Far East, the Garrs had unfinished business with the Burning Bush in Chicago. On their way to the East Coast, they stopped to meet with their former associates to mend any fences they could, but with an additional purpose. They wanted to inform Duke Farson and Edwin Harvey of their need to be baptized in the Holy Spirit, just as the Garrs had at Azusa Street.

Severing Ties That Bind

It is difficult to determine what kind of reception Alfred and Lillian expected in Chicago. In their estimation they had been powerfully impacted by a soon to sweep the world revival. Farson and Harvey had a different perspective. The Garrs had just shut down the Burning Bush congregation in Los Angeles and merged it with a much smaller one. Instead of salvaging the work they were sent to save, they had effectively ended the Burning Bush's West Coast operations. The Garrs might have expected a battle, but believing they had received "apostolic power" at Azusa Street, they were possibly expecting to convert the Burning Bush leadership to the new experience.

After arriving in Chicago, the Garrs found that other Burning Bush leaders had been invited to their meeting with Harvey and Farson. In fact this meeting was opened to anyone within the Burning Bush "family" who wanted to examine and judge the effects of the Azusa Street revival for themselves. R.L. Erickson, a current and future associate of Alfred Garr, made the trip along with his family. His daughter Hannah recalls the meeting, even though she was only a young child.

> *My father went to Chicago and we met the Garrs there. I'll never forget we had prayer, and Dr. Garr prayed in tongues. He scared the daylights out of us! Oh, he prayed! Oh, I can hear him! And we kids felt like we had to get under the chairs and my father didn't understand it.*

This account from young Hannah Erickson accurately summed up the experience of the Burning Bush family at the meeting. The children were impressed and amazed by the tongues—the adults were not. None at the Burning Bush meeting believed what the Garrs had received was valid, nor even understood it.

In all probability, the Garrs were unable to espouse a coherent theology surrounding the baptism of the Holy Spirit, so they were unable to convert anyone. Most leaders within the Holiness movement believed they were already baptized in the Holy Spirit, so the Garrs' claim was not only confusing, it was provocative. In fact, this meeting served to solidify Harvey and Farson's belief that Alfred had fallen into error.

The Final Decision

Some time earlier, after his Holy Spirit baptism and closing of the church, Alfred's name had quickly and quietly disappeared from *The Burning Bush* magazine. Although Harvey and Farson had not publicly censured him then, they had removed him from their national leadership team. After this meeting in Chicago, they denounced him—publicly of course.

> *A couple who we knew passed through Chicago recently. When we saw them before, they had shining faces, the oil of gladness, and the mighty power of the Holy Ghost upon their souls. Everywhere they went revivals were in evidence.*
>
> *Their eyes have now lost the luster and the shine is out of their faces. The poor folks had a burned out, hollow look and as they would speak, would suddenly break forth in this "unknown tongue," etc...we cannot in any sense accept these poor powerless backsliders and wanderers from God as exponents of any improvement on what Luther and Wesley and Fox had when they turned the world upside down...*
>
> *But the people whom we have met who say they have the gift of tongues, we believe have lost God and have run out of the paths of righteousness and are thousands of miles away from apostolic power.*
>
> *The reader will notice the absence of the name of Rev. A.G. Garr from among our workers. He has recently been led away by the people known in Los Angeles as the "Tongues" people, who profess to receive unknown tongues as an evidence of a third*

blessing. We have refrained from giving this notice to our readers until we could make an intelligent report of his exact condition.

From a close study of the man and his experience, we are forced to inform our readers that, instead of having an advanced experience and more power as he thinks he has, the light has left the eye, the fire is gone and we can see clearly that he has lost the Holy Ghost.

It now remains for the devil to give him more "light" and further "blessings," etc. until the poor man will wake up and find his boat wrecked and his soul lost. Brother Garr made a valiant fight against unrighteousness, but in his intense desire to see signs and wonders has evidently become dissatisfied with the old time power that redeems men from sin and destruction. It is with great personal regret we record this downfall of a man of good gifts and success as a soul winner.

Although Alfred and his mentor Shepard were reconciled, we have no information on any restoration between Alfred and Shepard's wife, whom Alfred had called a perfect devil. Assuming they were not reconciled, it appears God wanted Alfred to understand the power of his words and their effects on others. If he did not understand this through Holy Spirit conviction, he found out by being on the other end of the poison pen.

Alfred was publicly denounced by his former associates, without any opportunity to respond to their accusations. The editorial literally stated that he had "lost the Holy Ghost." Alfred was quickly learning humility and understanding the price required to walk in greater authority. But more humility was waiting.

Refused the Hand of Fellowship

After leaving Chicago, the Garrs traveled to Kentucky and visited Alfred's family, most of whom knew the Lord by now. After rehearsing to them the events of the last several months, Alfred decided to visit Asbury College. His plan was to meet with another notable leader of the Holiness movement—the president of Asbury College. Although rebuffed by the Burning Bush leaders, Alfred hoped to bring "Pentecost" to Asbury College, and he went straight to the top.

As mentioned earlier, Alfred and Lillian had both attended Asbury for a year and were well acquainted with the president. Lillian's father was a prominent Methodist pastor and a board member of Asbury and Alfred had been mentored by Dr. Hughes during his time as a student. But after joining the Burning Bush movement, Alfred had written a stinging criticism of his former mentor.

The Burning Bush often attacked prominent leaders within the ranks of the Holiness movement through their writings. But as a new editor of their magazine, Alfred soon distinguished himself by taking this writing technique to new heights, or actually greater lows. He had written the following piece about Dr. Hughes in early 1905.

> *Nearly everywhere the Burning Bush evangelists go nominal church members begin to fight dancing and leaping...a curse comes upon them for fighting God's Word and work, as in the case of J.W. Hughes of Asbury College... While I was in school there, he fought demonstration and called it the work of the devil. The night of which I speak we had one of the most powerful meetings I had attended up to that time and God was wonderfully in it; but afterwards Mr. Hughes pronounced it the work of the devil, and of course that grieved God.*

> *If he were not already backslidden, he backslid then. One could see that he grieved the Lord and lost the power, for he was so absorbed in the work of the new college building that the students were grieved on account of his lack of spirituality. He began allowing the students to go to the state college at Lexington, Ky., one of the most wicked places in the state, and there they became*

much like the students in that worldly college and even wore the same kind of uniforms, etc.

Things seemed to go from bad to worse until Mr. Hughes could get along with but few of his teachers; even the oldest one was compelled to leave him, and then most of the students left the school. He then had trouble with his children and God only knows what is going on in Asbury today as a result of this.

Surely God means what He says in regard to the dancing question and those who fight it are fighting against God. Poor Mr. Hughes! I am sorry that he is backslidden from God. May God open his eyes and show him that he has lost the Holy Ghost. God led me away from Asbury college, and unconsciously to myself, led me into the crowd of holy people in Chicago known as the Burning Bush, and glory to God, I see the true light as never before. I am still thanking God that there is freedom in Christ Jesus our Lord.

During his time with the Burning Bush, Alfred was discipled in some wonderful and terrible ways. He learned faith and sacrificial living in real life situations, but he also was infected with a terrible sectarian spirit. So profound was it, he felt completely comfortable at times, issuing the final assessment of someone's spirituality or holiness.

It is difficult to reconcile that Alfred Garr would write this scathing rebuke of Dr. Hughes, since we see him as the humble man who submitted himself and his congregation to another, smaller congregation. But upon closer examination, most leaders are strong-willed and make some fairly common mistakes arising from their temperament.

Alfred was a strong-willed leader and God had to bend and shape him for greater purposes. Paul, the writer of most of the New Testament, was equally as strong-willed, as were Peter, John, and most of the other apostles. God often chooses even those with anger problems, like Moses, and then reworks their nature in love and humility. This was the process of most apostles in the New Testament, and pretty much holds true in modern times as well.

Another common attribute of strong leaders is forward thinking, which makes it possible that Alfred had forgotten writing this piece. But from his report of their meeting, apparently Dr. Hughes had not.

> *After God had blessed me with the baptism of the Holy Spirit I went to visit the president of the college I had attended. How I did love that man! He had been very good to me when I was in college, and we had many good times together.*
>
> *This time his attitude was different; he was not as cordial as he had been formerly. I began to tell him what the Lord had done for me. He had heard it already. In my interest in telling the story, I drew closer and closer to him. Finally he threw out his hands and cried: "Stop! Don't come at me with that thing. I don't want that thing so close to me!"*

Whether Dr. Hughes was reacting based on negative reports about the Pentecostal outpouring or his memory of Alfred's stinging criticism, we cannot tell. Regardless, the outcome was identical as in Chicago. Alfred was no longer welcome at Asbury College. He had now been rejected by some of the best of the Holiness movement.

Returning to Danville

With past mentors and associates rejecting them, the Garrs left Kentucky and returned to the only place they could—Danville, Virginia. Although they had left there only six months previous, that half-year had been more than eventful; it was revolutionary. Alfred Garr was returning to the East Coast dramatically different than when he had left it.

For the previous couple of years, the Garrs had considered Danville their home. They had agonized over their decision to leave for Los Angeles and would not have gone, except the Burning Bush leaders had basically required it. Now as they returned, the Garrs anticipated trouble from the Burning Bush headquarters.

Accordingly, they sent word ahead, warning the Danville congregation of possible accusations. They also had the foresight to seek protection for their belongings as well. Alfred sent the following letter to Jim Sink, an elder in the congregation.

> *Dear Brother Sink:*
>
> *Do not move from the Slaughter House (Missionary Home) until you hear from me. We may come back to Danville before long.*
>
> *We are not in the Burning Bush anymore as Brother Farson has thought best to dismiss us on account of difference in doctrine between us. Try to hold things together until you hear from me again.*
>
> *All that furniture there is in my name, and I put it in your charge to hold for me, until I come. You will read the letter from Sister Garr to Sister Lillian which will explain things more fully. Keep praying for us that God may open the way for us to come to Danville soon if it be His will.*
>
> *We are in good spirits and are walking on with God as never before. May God bless and keep you true.*
> *As ever,*
> *A.G. Garr.*

Confirming the Faithful

The Garrs were unsure of what they would find upon returning to the Danville congregation. They had found little success introducing the Pentecostal blessing on their travels east, but the Burning Bush and Asbury leaders had reasons to be unreceptive. The Danville congregation was decidedly more open, but even the reception there would not be unanimous to this new experience.

When the Garrs arrived, they found the condition of the congregation worse than expected. Although their primary purpose was preparing for their missionary venture, Alfred was quick to deal with the trouble they encountered, and quick to introduce the Pentecostal experience he and Lillian received at the Azusa Street Mission.

> We are making preparations to go to India as soon as possible. Three of us, with the baby, four in all—will go just as soon as possible, so as to be on the ocean in the right time.

> ...we found the band to whom we had preached while here before, most of them backslidden and fussing among themselves. But when they saw that God had really done something wonderful for us, they all came in and began to seek the Lord. Most of them have been reclaimed and quite a number have been baptized with the Holy Ghost and have received the foreign tongue.

Again the early Pentecostals believed that the tongues being given were "missionary languages" for preaching the gospel in other lands. Alfred taught the Danville congregation to expect this. Alfred goes on in his article to explain.

> One girl received the baptism Friday night and she spoke in German. God sent us a German to interpret. He said he could understand everything perfectly. Sister Jennie Evans has also received the German language, and speaks it very fluently.

> Sister Garr improves every day in her Tibetan and Chinese.

Alfred continues in this article by describing the revival atmosphere that accompanied his time in Danville.

> The folks fall under the power of God, and a great time is on here. The church was packed twice yesterday and the altar over-flowing with seekers...a real revival has begun and three Holiness preacher boys have fallen in line. Two of them have received the baptism and the tongues...

> The sick are being healed. Soon after we arrived, a lady sick with dropsy came to the meeting. She got out of bed to come—had been sick a long time. As she told us how glad she was to see us

back in Danville and of her long sick spell, I said: "God will heal you" and took her hand. She immediately shouted that she was healed. I felt the healing power flow into her body. The next day she told us that her limbs had been swollen, but that every bit of it was driven out at once. She walked down town and then told her neighbors about the wonderful things the Lord had done for her.

Several have been healed. But, best of all many are getting the light, and as the Bible opens to us, they rejoice for the precious truths that have been hidden from us for so long by the "traditions of the elders." This is the greatest power I ever saw. I have wanted just this for years but did not know how to get it. After all, the great God opened my eyes and let me see the truth, and it liberated me from the bondage of ignorant teaching and the devil in general. I see the Bible now as never before.

Although the Lord moved in significant ways, the reception was not universal. Not all of the flock at Danville were convinced and entered into the Pentecostal blessing.

Many are tied through fear. Some are afraid of their leaders, some of one another, some are so afraid of third blessing that they are not quite so sure of the second…We rejoice daily that we are free from sectarianism. Hallelujah, that God ever showed us that there was a real witness to the baptism.

A Different Take

While the Garrs provide glowing reports from the Danville meetings, the Burning Bush headquarters took a different view. They had sent emissaries to Danville immediately after meeting with Alfred and Lillian in Chicago. They attempted to persuade the congregation to continue on the "path of righteousness," which meant staying with the Burning Bush.

But it appears they were unable to counter Alfred's influence with the congregation. He had planted the church and they were largely loyal to him, knowing his heart and manner of life. The Burning Bush leadership decided it was best to cut their losses short. Those willing were offered passage to the Burning Bush community in Waukesha. *The Burning Bush* provides their take on Danville in an article.

> *The sum and substance of the branch of this "tongues" that we have seen is that these people backslid no doubt, wishing to be the head of some kind of a work, and at once separated from the Burning Bush, and fearful lest this new god could not arrange for them a place of shelter, they immediately propose to seize the old barracks where they thought their friends were lodged, and, unknown to the Burning Bush leaders, capture the Danville work, by means of certain hands that they thought would be at the front and assist them, and thus secure for themselves a certain lodging place.*

> *We sent down immediately and sold off some of the principal articles of furniture that never were in Mr. Garr's name and turned them into cash, providing railroad fare for such of the folks as had salvation; put every one that would come on the train and brought them on to our school, as we felt after years of effort and successful work in the winning of souls that doubtless our work in this immediate vicinity was at an end for the present...*

> *The strange thing is that those who were formerly at enmity with Mr. Garr in his work are now the prominent ones in his meetings. The ones in whose spirituality he had no confidence when he really had the Lord, are now "speaking in tongues."*

The Burning Bush had built much of their following through denouncing other ministers and presenting themselves as "true Christian leaders." Harvey and Farson viewed Garr's inclusion of formerly hostile ministers as an indictment against his Pentecostal experience.

But Alfred had been freed from sectarianism at Azusa Street and was reconciled with other ministers in Danville whom he had once denounced. The Burning Bush considered this inclusiveness as evidence of Alfred's own backslidden condition, while Alfred understood that God was restoring him to right fellowship with the larger body of Christ.

A Final Attempt

Remarkably Harvey and Farson made a final attempt to draw Alfred and Lillian back into their fold. The Garrs had traveled to New York in preparation for their mission and R.L. Erickson was sent to persuade the Garrs to return to the Burning Bush. Although he neither understood nor agreed with the Garrs's new experience, Erickson was still a friend of the Garrs and was the perfect instrument of reconciliation.

Erickson traveled by train to New York and brought his family to meet with Alfred and Lillian, who had their young daughter with them. Alfred agreed to meet with Erickson on a train he was traveling on and even brought lunch for their meeting—tongue sandwiches.

We gain a glimpse of Alfred Garr that is often excluded from historical biographies. He was a fun loving man. He had no intention of rejoining the Burning Bush, but was happy to see the Ericksons, whom he considered friends. So he communicated in a "tongue in cheek manner" that to remain in fellowship with him, the Ericksons would have to be willing to endure "tongues."

Faith Instead of Safety

Continuing their preparation for India, Alfred and Lillian assessed their recent transformation. Stripped of success, reputation, relationships, and most of their possessions, they realized God was refining their faith, so they could trust Him alone. Instead of resisting or resenting this stripping, they chose to participate with the Lord and cultivate a deeper dependence on Him.

Before they left the States, a friend from the Holiness movement offered to cover any expenses they incurred in India and China. But after careful consideration, Alfred refused the offer, realizing that accepting it would be trusting in man instead of God.

> *A kind lady in the States told us before leaving there that she would support us on our trip, and all we needed to do was to write her when we needed anything. After praying about it we saw that if we took such an offer we would not have an opportunity to prove God's greatness and care. So we told her we would trust God only. We could not accept her kind offer but were thankful just the same.*

Alfred and Lillian had been trained in enduring hardship through their involvement with the Burning Bush. As evangelists they were accustomed to living on little as they pioneered the gospel and planted churches. However, there was always a financial safety net. The Burning Bush headquarters often covered the shortfalls of unprofitable evangelistic enterprises. But now Alfred and Lillian would venture forth without that assurance. Alfred felt if they could trust the Lord for finances, they could trust Him for anything.

Called into Question

One final safety net which was being torn, if not removed was the validity of their "apostolic languages." During this season Alfred met Arthur Payne, a furloughed missionary, who had served in India and spoke Hindi, a sister language to Bengali. After Alfred explained his Pentecostal experience and then speaking in his "apostolic language," Payne questioned its authenticity. Payne informed Alfred that he was most definitely not speaking any Indian dialect.

> *I have always regarded it as providential that I was allowed to meet the first Pentecostal missionary who went to India from the United States. A mutual friend introduced me to the missionary and he proceeded to speak to me in tongues.*

I then told him that I knew Hindi, a sister language, and that had he been speaking to me in Bengali, I must have understood at least a word, but did not do so and added it was impossible for me to believe that he was speaking Bengali at all. He replied he was quite certain he had…and had been told so by two Indian boys he had met in America.

His wife, who was present and who seemed quite a bright Christian woman had, both she and her husband assured me, received the gift of the Chinese language…earnest sincere people, but undoubtedly fanatical."

Alfred was now being tested on a key foundation of his new experience and theology. Trusting God for provision, new relationships, and his reputation was relatively easy for someone who had pioneered as the Garrs had previously. But now the validity of his experience was called into question by someone with no axe to grind. Had he really received apostolic languages, and if not, had he really received apostolic power? Time would tell.

Consecration, Testing, Victory, and Power

John G. Lake once observed there was a difference between being *filled with the Spirit* and being *in the power of the Spirit*. From Luke chapter 4 he noted this distinction is mentioned from Jesus' life.

> **Then Jesus, being filled with the Holy Spirit, returned from the Jordan and was led by the Spirit into the wilderness. Then Jesus returned in the power of the Spirit to Galilee…(Luke 4:1,14).**

Jesus was filled with the Holy Spirit when He was baptized by John in water. He then departed into the desert being filled with the Spirit. However, after forty days of fellowship with the Father and His subsequent testing by Satan in the wilderness, He returned in the power of the Holy Spirit. Lake realized that after being filled with the Spirit at His baptism, Jesus encountered testing, gained victory through dependence on His father, and came forth with power.

Alfred and Lillian Garr endured similar preparations as early Pentecostal missionaries. They were tested financially, relationally, and with false accusations. With each victory there were lessons learned and power provided. The power would be released very soon as they launched forth from the shores of America to India and beyond. But more testing would be waiting upon their arrival.

CHAPTER SIX

INTO THE FIELDS

After a brief stop in England, the Garrs arrived in India with their faith high. They excitedly walked off the ship only to discover their luggage had been stolen. They had refused all human support for their mission while in America, and now they had lost almost everything they owned. Alfred and Lillian Garr landed in India with $22.50 in their pockets.

They had little time to worry, for they had to get moving. The Garrs quickly rented a flat in the native section of Calcutta and moved in. Since they had very few of their belongings left, unpacking was not much of an issue.

Praying Through

Provision was an issue however. The Garrs had their young daughter Virginia with them and Maria Gardner had come along to help with her care. They had no fallback plan, so they examined the resources at their disposal. They had no mission board in the United States to support them and no personal contacts in India.

Alfred, Lillian, and Virginia Garr, Maria Gardner and other co-workers

Alfred and Lillian had been prepared for situations like this through their time in the Burning Bush. Two of the greatest lessons learned during the last five years were: trusting God for provision and the power of prayer. They needed both now. Alfred writes:

The devil tempted me much because I had no money and would point to my wife and baby and tell me that they would not be cared for. But after a hard fight on this line the Lord gave me the victory, and I have not been troubled on that point since.

Alfred, like most of the early Pentecostals, had nothing other than his faith in God. As a result he developed the habit of *praying through* whenever confronted with obstacles. They believed most battles were spiritual and were fought in the spirit realm and their own souls. Prayer was their main weapon.

When Alfred had written that *"after a hard fight...the Lord gave me the victory"* he meant he gained assurance in his soul that God would meet their financial needs. It was their custom to pray until they had this assurance in their heart. When it came, they knew the Lord had heard and would answer them. They did not need to see an outward change in their circumstances, just an inward change in their heart.

The Right Time and Place

Reports of the Azusa Street outpouring in Los Angeles had gone around the world the previous summer and had piqued the interest of many believers, especially among ministers and missionaries. But the reports of the strange behavior in the revival had also caused concern.

Alfred's ministry had previously been marked by God's ordained timing and placement such as their arrival in Los Angeles the same month as William Seymour. Their church facility had also been less than two miles from the Azusa Street Mission. This grace followed them onto the mission field.

The Garrs arrived in India a few weeks prior to missionaries from across India who were arriving in Calcutta for prayer gatherings. For a number of reasons, many of the Christian leaders there were expecting God to move powerfully during this season. Alfred and Lillian attended these prayer meetings and recognized that God had ordained the timing and the place.

*We found them waiting in prayer when we reached Calcutta,
though they had no idea that God would do as Peter recorded of
the Gentiles...*

*After waiting upon the Lord for three weeks, God in a
marvelous way opened a "door of utterance" for us in Calcutta
at the Lall Bazaar Baptist Church, the remodeled church in
which Adonirim Judson, the great missionary to Burma preached
forth the first time in India.*

*Amid marble busts of pioneer missionaries... The missionaries
were congregated in Calcutta, then the seat of government...the
viceroy was in...the missionaries...were waiting on God...
We found them hungry and receptive; the soil was broken...*

Alfred did not preach during this gathering, but he met most of
the missionaries. Knowing that he had come from the Los Angeles
outpouring, a number of rumors soon emerged about the strange
manifestations and the tongues phenomenon which accompanied their
ministry. A Presbyterian minister, Max Moorhead, met with Alfred
to discuss these rumors.

*A Calcutta resident, a prominent Christian worker said to me
one day. "Mr. and Mrs. Garr are devoted and earnest Christian
people but in regard to the tongue question they are not on Bible
lines, hence they need instruction: Will you help them?" Feeling
sorry that such earnest souls had imbibed erroneous doctrine, I
promised to endeavor to lead them into the truth, an accordingly
called to see them in their lodgings where I was cordially received.*

*I learned after I came to know them better that they had
witnessed some very stirring scenes in California...Not only had
they been eye witnesses to the Latter Rain outpouring of the Holy
Spirit as on the Day of Pentecost, but they had personally received
the baptism of the Holy Ghost with signs following (Acts 2:4).*

Before leaving Brother Garr's lodgings, we knelt together in prayer, and while he was praying, the Spirit spoke supernaturally through his lips, in tongues. His utterance caused me to feel a sense of awe in the majesty of his presence, and in my heart I worshiped...

As I walked away meditating upon the wondrous things which I had seen and heard, I had completely forgotten that the object of my visit was to put Brother Garr on right lines! Indeed it began to dawn upon me that perhaps after all I was the one who needed to get on Bible lines.

Alfred was already being examined for his beliefs and he had yet to preach one sermon. This episode foreshadowed two things that would follow Alfred for the next decades: persecution arising from accusations and success which came from his sincerity and demonstration of supernatural power.

An Open Door

A number of significant leaders among the missionaries gathered in Calcutta were also touched by Alfred's testimony during these "days of waiting." Again Max Moorhead provides insight:

Among others who received the testimony of Mr. and Mrs. Garr concerning the baptism in the Holy Ghost according to Acts 2:4 was Pastor Hook of the Carey Baptist Chapel who invited the Garrs to hold meetings in his place of worship in Bow Bazaar. Nearly all of the missionaries and workers...received the testimony concerning Pentecost, and began to tarry for "The promise of the Father."

It was only fitting that the first Pentecostal missionary sent out from the Azusa Street revival started his mission in the Indian church founded by William Carey, father of modern missions. Max Moorhead provides more insight about these meetings and his own perspective.

Constitutionally of a cautious nature, I did not purpose to plunge headfirst into an enterprise which might prove to be fanatical. Early in January 1907 when my friends were gathered in this chapel to seek the Lord in His fullness, I held aloof, because I desired to consider from all sides this tongues phenomenon.

One day while walking alone, I said, "Lord, please keep me out of error and fanaticism." Then He spoke to my mind and heart, quieting my alarms, and directing my attention to the Bible, His Spirit assuring my heart that the glorious baptism was just what I needed, and that I might safely seek the fullness which there is in Jesus.

Alfred began preaching in this congregation on January 13, 1907. These meetings were marked by deep conviction of sin on the part of Christians and the unsaved. Max Moorhead continues the narrative.

Having opportunity, day by day, to observe closely the Spirit's manifestations, I discovered the shallowness of much popular criticism and by examining the Word of God my faith was greatly strengthened...

*On the evening of the 15th of January 1907, Brother Garr gave an address upon the theme "Abiding in Christ"... There was to me nothing new or original in his remarks, **but the demonstration of the Spirit which immediately followed his words was tremendous. A spirit of conviction of sin fell upon several members of that little company.***

A lady present confessed that she had defrauded the Customs Department. A British soldier was vividly reminded of a theft he had committed in the past; he promised restitution. A confession from the lips of a young Indian was of a very wicked deed: the Spirit seemed as if He were to wring the humbling admission of sin from his lips.

Pungent conviction and open confession of sin is one of the leading characteristics of the Spirit's work in India.

But there were other demonstrations of the Spirit that accompanied Alfred's ministry and messages as well. And this was extremely upsetting to those more accustomed to solemn meetings. Max Moorhead continues.

> At times sounds of holy hilarity and laughter would be heard and the saints would even reel and stagger as if intoxicated. Others related visions and dreams…fell into trances…the preaching was…followed by such shrieks and groans on the part of some of the auditors that it seemed as if they could see and hear the torment of damned souls in hell…

> The report of the speaking in tongues and prostrations brought many people, some of whom were convicted and blessed and others who scoffed and ridiculed…

Alfred had found the door of utterance that he had prayed for and was seeing success, but their other prayer focus had seen no answer. Their financial needs were still looming. Although Alfred had received an assurance of the Lord's provision in his soul, nothing had changed in his wallet.

Faith and Experience Rewarded

Then God did something wonderful. A British military officer requested an audience with Alfred at the church facility. Captain Angelsmith told Alfred that God had burdened him for the missionaries and handed Alfred a bag full of gold coins.

Apparently before Captain Angelsmith had left England for India, he was instructed by the Lord to set aside his tithes until further instruction. For eight months he had saved his tithes, and waited on God's direction. Captain Angelsmith gave them this money, and it covered their expenses for their entire Indian mission.

This grace for finances was an aspect of Alfred's ministry that distinguished him from many early Pentecostal missionaries. According to some historical accounts, many of the earliest Pentecostal missionaries, with no board to support them, became wards of other missionary groups until they received money to return home. Some had jumped into the field with much zeal, but little experience or backing.

In many cases, their failure was due to an inability to raise financial support. Others had so little experience in ministry that they were simply unable to endure on the mission field. Others struggled or failed because their "apostolic languages" did not prove true. Believing that they had been empowered to speak native tongues, most were devastated when they were unable to do so on the field.

Avoiding the Paralysis of Analysis

The confusion over apostolic languages could have discouraged Alfred as well. He had spoken in an Indian dialect while in Los Angeles, which had been confirmed by those who knew the language. Lillian had also spoken in Chinese when she was baptized in the Holy Spirit. But they had no ability to speak these languages when they arrived on the field.

Alfred had suspected en route that he might not be able to speak the Indian dialects when he arrived in India. He was not completely sure what to think about this, but he was sure about what he had experienced. He realized God had used the Indian dialects that he had spoken in Los Angeles to direct them to India. But he wondered about the apostolic languages aspect of the gift of tongues.

He began to examine the Scriptures for a clearer explanation of tongues and their purpose in a believer's life. His examination revealed several passages that helped Alfred formulate what would become the classical Pentecostal understanding of the initial evidence of the Holy Spirit baptism.

Alfred discovered that although the apostles had spoken in other languages on the Day of Pentecost, this ability did not continue with them throughout their lives. He also discovered the various passages about speaking mysteries (see I Corinthians 14:2); edifying yourself (see I Corinthians 14:4); and building yourself in faith through praying in tongues (see Jude 20).

His understanding of tongues from the Scripture was published in a pamphlet he printed and distributed in March 1907, while in India. This pamphlet, *Pentecostal Power*, was distributed widely in the United States and in India. Historian Gary McGee credits Alfred and his pamphlet, with formulating the classical Pentecostal position on the purpose of tongues in a believer's life.

Humility in Success

The Garrs, like other Pentecostal pioneers, did not understand everything about this new experience, but they were sure of what it had provided them—power from God as witnesses. They possessed a deep burden for the lost and God had given them new power for winning them. And that was worth enduring the humility of not completely understanding everything about what they had received.

Alfred also kept his success in perspective. While others saw him as a successful and ground-breaking missionary, he saw himself as a sinner continually in need of God's grace at all times. In a letter to his family written during the spring of 1907, he reports on his Indian mission. He discussed their success and the requests that come from every quarter.

> *All praise and honor to Jesus. I am unworthy of all his mercies. Only by His grace am I able to speak...May God help us to see the pressing need of His grace in us each moment, saving us from all sin; the sin of anger, pride, neglect of prayer; real earnest prayer, and neglect of His precious Bible.*

Alfred did not just preach to others about their need for God, he modeled his own need of Him. In addition to revival meetings in the evenings, prayer and seeking meetings were held during the day. Alfred led many of these meetings and was seeking God himself, not just encouraging others to do so. He maintained and modeled spiritual hunger.

A Change of Venue

After three months in Calcutta, the Garrs relocated their base to Bombay for the remainder of their Indian mission. During that time they ministered at two other significant gatherings. The first was in Conoor which was another gathering place for missionaries. His meetings there were effective, but very controversial, and much persecution resulted.

Now the accusation that had simmered began boiling. Different Holiness and Missionary magazines published a number of articles questioning the Garrs' teaching and practice. Almost all of these articles reported the Garrs were sincere but deceived people. Remarkably, these accounts, although questioning the Pentecostal experience, reported that God did work through the Garrs' ministry.

They also traveled to a famous mission led by an Indian national, Pandita Ramabai. She had heard about the Pentecostal outpouring and requested the Garrs come to her mission. Before Alfred could get there, the Lord baptized several hundred of them in the Holy Spirit.

When Alfred arrived at the mission, he focused on strengthening their work and preparing them for the inevitable persecution and withdrawal of support that would follow. Alfred's experience and wisdom helped prepare Pandita and her mission for the transition they had entered.

To the Orient

Alfred and Lillian had originally left the United States with the intention of traveling to both India and China. During their time in Conoor they were impressed strongly that the time had arrived for them to go to China. They prayed for provision and God answered quickly.

Alfred and Lillian Garr third row on the left. Virginia Garr front row third from left.
Mok Lai Chi, on the second row center, Pentecostal Mission of Hong Kong, 1907

> *When we were sure that God wanted us to leave India for*
> *China, we said, yes Lord, we will go as soon as the money is*
> *provided. We took no collection and did no begging, but within*
> *four days or so after we told the Lord we would come, the money*
> *came to us.*

On October 8, 1907, the missionary party arrived in Hong Kong. Their belongings made it this time. Alfred's grace of divine timing continued and included the arrival of co-workers to help, since Lillian was now pregnant with their second child. May Law and Rose Pittman, two young missionaries from the United States, arrived in Hong Kong, the same day Alfred began meetings and quickly joined their efforts.

Within two days, Alfred had secured the local congregational church, called the American Board Church Mission, pastored by a Dr. Hager, to host meetings. May Law stated:

Dr. Hager had had trouble in the church with the Chinese members over the building, and after the service on the Sunday prior to this, he declared to his wife he would never preach there again until things were settled, so when the Garrs came asking if they could have the church for special meetings, he threw the door wide open and told them to go ahead, so the services were already in progress when we arrived.

Immediate Success

They began their Hong Kong ministry on the second day after their arrival and spent the first month preaching the need for repentance and the restitution. Alfred reports:

In two days a large building was opened and from four hundred to seven hundred Chinese came to the services, and most every Sabbath evening the house was filled, even the aisles to within six feet of the pulpit.

The pattern was much the same as in India. His preaching blended the standards of righteousness and the love of God. Crowds were there from the beginning and the meetings were quickly successful. Once again the Spirit of God visited with deep conviction of sin. Believers and unbelievers publicly confessed their sins and made restitution.

Alfred had either developed a unique ability to gather both believers and unbelievers, or it was simply a grace from God. He believed that both sinner and saint needed a deeper touch from God and his preaching was able to capture both at the same time. Just as in India, many were most impressed by the conviction which accompanied Alfred's preaching.

An owner of an English school and leader in a local church, Mok Lai Chi was profoundly touched. He was so impressed by the quality and depth of repentance and brokenness that people experienced, he reevaluated his past success in light of the current revival. In his testimony he wrote that:

Before Brother Garr came, I spent all my time in the mission work, besides my school hour, and yet I have not seen one man who really repented...

By Christmas, Alfred and Lillian were experiencing even greater success as more believers were baptized in the Holy Spirit and many unbelievers found the Lord. However, they soon had to leave the American Board Mission and began to look for another facility.

Immediately Mok Lai Chi offered his school facility to the Garrs and began assisting Alfred in the ministry there. This was the birth of the Pentecostal Mission of Hong Kong. By January the meetings continued accelerating in power and attendance was increasing even more.

Persecution Increases

However, persecution became success' companion. With believers and unbelievers being touched profoundly, persecution arose from both places as well. Criminals and hooligans began trying to interrupt the meetings. In addition, Alfred wrote about the increasing persecution from the church in this letter published in the *Bridegroom's Messenger*:

It is a hard fight here at times. The devil is making it quite interesting for us of late; God however is taken by us, and the work goes on.

I praise God that in Los Angeles, God put me to the test before I was baptized with His Spirit; and I know that I died to every friend...to my family and my church relationship, to what people would say about me the balance of my life.

I died to being called crazy and fanatical, while I had been called both before, yet God showed me that I would have to endure much more...

I am truly glad that you are standing true and not afraid to reveal which side you are on. It is cause for rejoicing to find a man that believes something and is not afraid to tell it...

One aspect of the apostolic calling that few discuss is the call to suffer. The Scriptures reveal that an apostle was marked for persecution and suffering for the sake of Christ and the gospel. Paul had received this as part of his mandate (see Acts 9:15-16) and the twelve were given this cup as well (see Mark 10:39). The Lord had shown Alfred that he, too, was called to suffer persecution as he fulfilled his ministry.

An apostle is called to pioneer the gospel and confront strongholds of unbelief. This often results in provocation, anger, unrighteous accusation, and slander from the powers that be. Although it is difficult on the minister who is the target—it serves the purposes of God because it provides "free advertising" for the gospel.

Prophetic Insight

In this same article Alfred revealed that he had received a prophetic impression concerning a shaking coming to the American Pentecostal movement.

> *While in prayer the other day, the Lord seemed to show me that the work in America was going to be put through a severe sifting in the near future; and that there would be many sifted out, because they will not be firm and very determined to go through it.*

> *Some are in the movement because it had a "sweep" when the power first fell, and they being swept in, when there was little or no persecution, will now, be sifted out during this time of trial that God will permit the church to pass through.*

Several weeks earlier, both he and Lillian had been impressed by God that they would be returning to the States before long. Both had felt that God was calling them back for a short season to strengthen the Pentecostal believers at home, but they were unsure about the timing.

Sorrow in the Midst of Joy

Aside from the continuing persecution, everything was going well for the Garrs. Their Hong Kong venture was blossoming and the work in India continued to grow. The church in Danville, Virginia was doing well in spite of their separation from the Burning Bush. The favor of God seemed to be on everything they touched.

But soon sorrow found their address. Lillian who was pregnant gave birth to a stillborn daughter. They named her Josephine after Alfred's mother. The Garrs were heartbroken, but their faith was unscathed. There is no evidence that either of them questioned God or had a crisis of faith.

On the contrary, in their sorrow, Alfred and Lillian were still thinking of others. They felt led to extend their parenting to May Law and Rose Pittman. These two young ladies were battling discouragement in their missions work and were currently losing the fight.

> One thing so precious to me was when we met the Garrs, she threw her arms around me and said, "Sister Pittman, I'll be a mother to you," and that she was, as long as she was there…The Lord spoke to Brother Garr that very afternoon after meeting us, and said, "I was a stranger and ye took me in." He said he knew at once the Lord wanted him to secure a house large enough to take us in, which he did, after a couple of weeks.

The Garrs brought them into their home and provided a shelter for them, both materially and spiritually. They discipled them in the life of faith and the endurance needed to thrive on the mission field. Both young ladies were profoundly impacted by the way God met their needs in response to the Garr's faith and prayers.

Worldwide Persecution

At this juncture, the Garrs had been used to pioneer the Pentecostal message and further the gospel in India, Ceylon, Hong Kong, and

China. As these works quickly grew, the persecution reached a new level. This excerpt is from an article printed in *The Independent*, a Holiness magazine.

It is a curious sight to see a company of the unemotional Chinese swept by this strange delusion, kneeling or prostrate on the ground, their eyes closed, their faces set in frenzied abstraction, pouring out for hours a stream of meaningless sounds. It is presumably a study in hysteria, for, in their publications, the converts report "hours of laughter," which they interpret as divine incitement...

The excitement began in South China with the arrival in Hong Kong last fall of a man named A.G. Garr and his wife, their three years old child, a Negro woman (whom the neighbors describe as "the best of the lot") and two young women.

Garr was from the Los Angeles center. He was formerly a railroad employee and a Methodist. He then passed into the "Burning Bush" order—a body certainly with scriptural warrant as regards to title. As to whether this brotherhood ejected him or he was not sufficiently spiritually fed, the gossips differ; but at all events he is now a shining light among the "Tongues" people...

He took quarters among the Chinese, and soon the meetings were attracting great crowds, including many who came to scoff, but did not remain to pray.

Garr dealt largely in abuse. The visitor entering the hall caught loud tones of denunciation, and when he retired some fine specimens of anathema followed him into the street, often with a personal application... The work has caused some division in these native churches, although there has been some abatement in the frenzy, and the Chinese, regretting their digression, are returning to their folds.

> *The meetings drew three hundred people night after night.*
> *Hundreds went under the spell, shaking and shouting in "tongues,"*
> *and in general conducting themselves like howling dervishes…*

The article continued by suggesting these manifestations were both heathen and demonic. This article was published by an anonymous writer and "verified" by the editor of *The Independent*. Other publications accused Alfred of spiritualism, hypnosis, emotionalism, and of simply being a fraud. Many of these were literally distributed around the world.

Sorrow Upon Sorrow

The next month, Alfred went into Canton, China to help two other missionaries launch a work there. The meetings lacked in power from the start. They decided to suspend them and seek God for clarity. After praying for some time, they felt to wait before the Lord for the gifts of the Spirit and power. Within two weeks they received direction to begin again.

Just as the meetings restarted, Alfred received a telegram from Lillian to return home at once. Tragedy had struck. Maria Gardner had contracted smallpox, and she died on March 20, 1908. Virginia, Alfred's only child died the next day. Lillian, who had cared for both, was also quite sick during this time either from a tumor or small-pox—the historical accounts differ. Regardless, the Lord pulled her through.

Two other workers in their mission also contracted smallpox and were quarantined on a ship in the harbor until their recovery. Everything in the missionary home had to be destroyed. Annie Kirby writes from Canton, April 6, 1908 regarding these events.

> *Brother Garr received a telegram from his wife in Hong Kong,*
> *to come at once. He hated to leave the meeting but felt he must go.*
> *The faithful colored sister, Maria, who went with them to India*

*and has proven so faithful and true, had smallpox and died.
While they were burying "Sister Maria," their only child, little
Virginia died. Oh, it was so sad for them.*

*They are very much in need of our earnest prayers. Sister
Garr is not at all well. Sisters Law and Pitman both have the
smallpox and are in a boat on the water, quarantined.*

The Garrs were accustomed to hardship, but this was a tragedy on
a different level. Until this, their confidence was strong. Their meetings
were successful and well attended. All of the works they had planted
were doing well. The Pentecostal movement was growing. Although
we have no record of their emotional state, they were probably somewhat confused when it appeared that the protection and favor of God
had disappeared overnight.

To make matters worse, the enemies of the Pentecostal movement
used this tragedy to prove that the Garr's message was not true. They
ridiculed the Garr's saying they could not endure missionary life. An
article in *The Independent* mocks them in their grief.

*The Garrs have gone home. Smallpox caused the death
of the poor old Negro woman and the Garrs' child, who was
neglected in life. And when the two young women were taken to
the pest ship in the harbor with the same disease, the Garrs quietly
boarded a steamer and went back to Japan, where are others of
the brotherhood, and probably returned to America. Of course,
the enthusiasts would have no medical attendance.*

*There is another group of these curious fanatics now in
Canton...McIntosh is at the head...He is cast in a gentler mold
than the authoritative Garr but his ignorance is so great that he
can read only simple English...*

Although Alfred and Lillian were planning to return stateside,
this probably sped their return. The work in Hong Kong was turned
over to Mok Lai Chi and another gentleman, T.M. Sung. Both of

these men had been involved almost from the inception of the mission. Alfred, and Lillian who was recovering slowly, boarded a ship for home.

Not Finished Yet

But they were not finished in the Orient yet. Whatever sorrow they carried from the deaths of their children and co-workers is not clear to us. What is clear is that Alfred would not stop his mission except at God's direction. God had already shown them they would soon return to the States, but the enemy or tragedy would not push him out of the field.

Instead, they stopped in Japan and ministered there for the better part of three months. Though they were still hurting from the deaths of their children and co-worker, God used them powerfully there. Stanley Frodsham, writing in 1916, reports on the remarkable impact they had during that brief trip.

> *The Lord did more in a few weeks through the Garrs in Japan than all we other Pentecostal missionaries have done in many years.*

Without our modern tools for travel or communication, Alfred and Lillian Garr had literally compassed the earth carrying the fires of the Pentecostal revival in less than two years. Now they were headed home unsure of what they would find.

CHAPTER SEVEN

REDEEMING THE TIME

Alfred and Lillian arrived in Los Angeles in late spring of 1908 and reacquainted themselves with friends and supporters. Alfred had maintained correspondence with William Seymour during their mission ventures and now visited the Azusa Street Mission again. But they had not returned to simply see friends and attend meetings.

As mentioned previously, the Lord had spoken to both of them that the Pentecostal movement would come under significant persecution in the United States. They had felt led to the United States to strengthen those who would be affected. At this time, Alfred and Lillian were uniquely positioned to encourage and challenge the emerging Pentecostals.

While in India and China, they had corresponded regularly with Pentecostal leaders throughout the United States. Many of their letters were published as "reports from the mission field." With their success and experiences documented and distributed through magazines such as Seymour's *The Apostolic Faith*, and *The Bridegroom's Messenger*, published by G.B. Cashwell, the Garrs were well known by name, if not by face to many Pentecostals.

A Kingdom Vacation

Before leaving Los Angeles, Alfred took a personal and ministry inventory. They had been very successful both in India and China. God had miraculously provided for them on the field. Their work continued to be strong in their absence. However, Alfred had lost two children, a co-worker and nearly his wife. Persecution also followed almost every success.

With this in their minds, Alfred and Lillian began their mission to North America. Over the next sixteen months, they compassed

North America doing exactly what they had planned—strengthening the young Pentecostal movement and spreading the burden for missions.

They traveled first to visit Alfred's family. His mother had passed away while they ministered in India and they had not seen Alfred's family since. While they were still in Kentucky, during the summer, Lillian's mother passed away. They traveled to Missouri to attend her memorial service and see other relatives. These were their only non-working trips.

Alfred lived by his personal motto of "Just get started." He believed anything worth doing was worth doing now. He had discovered that God would meet his faith, if he would be willing to get moving now, just as Abraham had done. Believing that the days were evil, he tried to "redeem the time"(see Ephesians 5:16).

They met with many Pentecostal leaders during this time, encouraging and strengthening them for the days of persecution they had been warned about. They met with A. J. Tomlinson, leader of the Church of God, in Cleveland, Tennessee. They traveled to Atlanta and met with G.B. Cashwell, editor of *The Bridegroom's Messenger*. They also conducted revival meetings during their travels.

Touching a Leader

While strengthening the young Pentecostals was their primary purpose in the United States, missionary ventures were never far from Alfred and Lillian's minds. They talked about missions whenever they spoke. They sought to mobilize others into missions and helped raise support for those currently serving on the field.

While ministering at the Oliver Gospel Mission in Columbia, South Carolina, Alfred received a prophetic word concerning a man who he had heard about, but had never met, Joseph H. King. King was the general overseer of the Fire Baptized Holiness Church, and lived in North Carolina. Alfred felt from the Lord that Dr. King was supposed to travel to the emerging Pentecostal centers around the world and help ground them in the Scriptures.

Not at all intimidated by not knowing him, or by how ridiculous it might appear to Dr. King, Alfred moved forward. He asked A.E. Robinson, one of the leaders of the Oliver Gospel Mission and a friend of Dr. King, to invite him to Columbia. We find this account in Dr. King's own words.

> *In the spring of 1909, I received an invitation from A.E. Robinson to visit Columbia, SC...Being quite busy with the three departments of work that I was conducting...I passed the matter off as of no consequence...I replied...that I had neither time nor money to come to Columbia.*
>
> *In a day or so I received another letter, agreeing to defray my traveling expenses if I should do so...Mr. and Mrs. Garr, Pentecostal missionaries from China, were visiting and laboring in Columbia... and very much desired to see me.*

Dr. King was not concerned with the financial cost as much as being away from his responsibilities, which were many. He was overseeing their movement, teaching in their school, editing a newsletter, and leading an orphanage. When it was decided he could leave Friday afternoon and return on Monday, he agreed to come.

> *I decided to accept...as I would not lose any time from the school. I knew nothing as to what was in the minds of Mr. and Mrs. Garr before leaving...Brother Robinson did not reveal this in the letters he wrote.*

Dr. King arrived late on Friday evening and met with Alfred, Lillian, and Rev. Robinson the next morning. After exchanging introductions and pleasantries, Alfred simply shared his prophetic impression. Dr. King wrote:

> *Mr. and Mrs. Garr informed me as to their conviction concerning my visiting Pentecostal centers in many foreign countries. Brother Robinson also gave it his unqualified endorsement. I at once informed them that it was not possible …*
>
> *I had opened the Falcon Orphanage [three months previous] … along with the work I was doing in the school, I decided that it would be a lack of loyalty to God…to go on a tour of the world…in fact it seemed a matter of foolishness to entertain the thought…I did not want to travel. This I had done, more or less, for eighteen years up to that time. I desired to settle down and rest from such a life…So the tour of the world was dismissed from my mind.*

With good reasons, Dr. King dismissed the idea almost immediately. He left their gathering with no intention of dropping his current work and traveling around the world. Alfred walked away from this meeting, after seeing his prophetic word rejected, and simply continued his ministry at the Oliver Gospel Mission.

However, that was not the end of the story. Skipping ahead several months we find that God soon began to change Dr. King's heart and mind. He continues this account.

> *As 1909 was coming to a close, I was made to consider very seriously the proposition of making the trip proposed in the spring by Mr. and Mrs. Garr. It forced itself upon my mind from day to day, and I was compelled to give it consideration.*
>
> *It became a burden so heavy that I could scarcely bear it. My sleep was disturbed and my waking hours distracted …*

Skipping forward a little more for this part of our story, Dr. King did eventually respond positively to this prophetic word from Alfred. In September 1910, he turned over all his current ministry responsibilities to others and embarked on a two-year teaching mission to the Pentecostal centers of the world, just as Alfred had suggested.

He traveled throughout India, Ceylon, China, Hong Kong, and the other nations the Garrs had visited. He also traveled to other nations and Pentecostal groups as well. He taught doctrinal foundations about the baptism of the Holy Spirit and other aspects of life in the Holy Spirit, helping biblically ground the emerging movement.

At that juncture, only the Lord knew that Pentecostal Christianity would become the fastest growing religious movement of the twentieth century. It was important that these new leaders become squarely grounded in the Word and also important for them to connect with someone who would have significant influence over the next decade.

Impacting a Movement

In January 1911, while his trip was just beginning, the Fire Baptized Holiness Church, overseen by Dr. King, merged with the Pentecostal Holiness Church, a Pentecostal denomination. Soon, as a result of Dr. King's teaching throughout the nations and Alfred's respect for him as a leader, a significant number of those associated with Alfred and Lillian joined the Pentecostal Holiness Church.

Within a few years of his return to the United States, Joseph King became the overseer of the Pentecostal Holiness Denomination and led them for over twenty years. To this day, the Pentecostal Holiness Church's missions program still ranks as one of the best organized and best funded groups in the world, thanks largely to the heart and effort of J.H. King.

It is important to note that the man who started the Pentecostal Holiness Church's mission thrust had effectively retired from traveling until he received a prophetic word from Alfred Garr. When he received this word, God put him on a course that would change many people and an entire denomination. By touching Joseph King, Alfred altered the course of a denomination.

This story illustrates another aspect of an apostolic life. Alfred, although a powerful minister and effective in many areas, recognized that to accomplish his task, he needed other's help. His goal was to establish the believers in God and all He had for them. He realized that it would take a diversity of ministries to do this and sought out others who could help.

Some ministers wrongly believe they are sufficient to meet all the needs of those they serve, but Alfred saw the need for other ministries, those different than his own. He was not concerned with maintaining his own reputation or special relationship with the flocks, he wanted them to be established in God. That would require the ministries of others in addition to his ministry.

Alfred understood, just as Paul, that his mandate was to plant and others would water the plantings after him (see I Corinthians 3:6-8). Alfred saw his part of the plan was only just that—a part. His desire was for the believers to be established, not his reputation. He wanted the believers to be established in God, regardless of who received credit.

The Center of Storms

Back to 1909—Alfred and Lillian remained in Columbia, South Carolina, for several months after their encounter with Dr. King. They were holding revival meetings at the Oliver Gospel Mission. This was a Holiness group who had significant influence nationally through their *Way of Faith* magazine. As a group they were mostly supportive of the Pentecostal movement.

However, some of their board members were unsure about tongues and other manifestations of the Holy Spirit. Appreciating the zeal which was released however, they had adopted a wait and see attitude toward the Pentecostal movement. They would not have to wait long to see something which caused them to make a decision.

Alfred's revival meetings were powerful and expressive. Soon people were speaking in tongues, being slain in the Spirit, jumping, dancing, and shouting during the meetings. At other times, confession of sin would be so loud and open that religious sensitivities were ruffled.

Some of the mission's board members did not appreciate the different manifestations of the Spirit and reactions of the people. Without going into great detail, the Oliver Gospel Mission and the *Way of Faith* effectively blew apart as a result of the controversy. The controversy was so inflammatory that the secular newspapers began reporting on it.

Although mentioned only briefly in the last chapter, a similar controversy had surrounded Alfred's ministry in Conoor, India. His meetings among the missionaries gathered there also produced many unusual manifestations and reactions. This was so controversial that it effectively split the Pentecostal movement in India.

In reality, both places had splits which were simmering before Alfred arrived. His ministry was such, however, that it demanded attention and provoked reactions. Paul wrote in I Corinthians 4:9 that apostles were like *spectacles on display* for the whole world to see. Alfred had this calling and it produced some severe reactions in response.

He was also a man in process at this time. His heart really was for unity and Christian love, but he also felt compelled to preach the uncompromising truth of God's Word. He had been so negatively affected by leaders who had compromised the Word during his childhood that he would not do the same to others.

He believed that tongues and other manifestations of the Holy Spirit were real and beneficial, so he would not compromise them. He realized that choosing respectability over the anointing of God, regardless of how foolish it appeared, was a dangerous precedent. He would preach the truth and deal with the consequences instead.

North of the Border

Alfred and Lillian traveled next to Toronto, in Ontario, Canada to participate in a camp meeting at Stouffville, near Ontario. These meetings were attended by most emerging leaders such as A.A. Boddy, Robert Semple and his young wife, Aimee.

It was during their time in Canada that Lillian began to emerge as a significant voice in Pentecostal circles. A.A. Boddy provides this report from the Stouffville camp meeting.

> *The Lord has poured out His Spirit upon the women. The women are breaking the alabaster box at Jesus' feet. The old long-necked cruse only dropped a drop at a time of the precious ointment. Mary wanted to break it, for she wanted the Lord to be generously supplied. Pentecost has cut many loose to give Him all they have and are, to pour out ungrudgingly, unstintingly.*

> *Brother and Sister Garr are Southerners, of a refined type. They are good-looking, well-made young people, fit to move in any society, but what voices they have when speaking in meetings! Mrs. Garr seems to be about six feet high and her voice would carry a great distance in the open air.*

Lillian shared about their experiences in India and Hong Kong. As she shared about the deaths of her daughters and their co-worker, Maria Gardner, the people were deeply moved by their sacrifice. A significant offering for missionaries serving in the field was received after Lillian spoke.

Over the next few years Lillian emerged as a tremendous teacher, complementing, and for a time eclipsing, Alfred's own ministry. Lillian, with no children to care for, began to emerge more fully into this role of teaching as they continued traveling across North America, stopping at Winnipeg in Manitoba, Canada, and then to Vancouver in British Columbia, Canada, where they again met and strengthened a number of leaders.

But the Garrs were not long in North America. They had accomplished their purpose of strengthening and encouraging the young Pentecostal movement. They had been here for almost eighteen months and now they traveled westward with purpose. They returned to Los Angeles in order to board a ship for Hong Kong and China. They had planned all along to return to the Orient and now the time was ripe.

Reoriented

Alfred and Lillian returned to Hong Kong early in the autumn of 1909. They arrived back in the country they had sown their young daughters into less than two years earlier. No co-workers traveled with them this time, because without children, Lillian needed no help.

When they arrived at the Pentecostal Mission of Hong Kong they found the work continuing *and* progressing. Remarkably, in spite of the persecution that had accompanied their success in Hong Kong, only one member of the mission had fallen away in their absence.

Also, Mok Lai Chi had stepped into the leadership role in a very effective fashion. He had not only maintained the work, he had also started an evangelistic outreach while the Garrs were in North America. Soon Alfred and Mok were involved in this evangelistic outreach while Lillian taught the believers in the Mission.

One week after arriving in Hong Kong, Alfred decided to open a missionary home. This would provide a vehicle to disciple and help support other missionaries, as they had done previously. They had seen remarkable fruit from sharing their home with May Law and Rose Pittman on their previous trip, and they believed it was essential to spreading the gospel into China.

Abased and Abounding

This took significant faith, because despite their continued success, financial support was reduced during this time in Hong Kong.

There were a number of reasons for this. First, the ongoing persecution and slander had caused some individuals to withdraw their financial support.

The second reason was actually a good problem. By this time, a number of other believers had emerged as Pentecostal missionaries. As they entered the field, they effectively taxed the existing support base, thereby reducing support for established missionaries.

The last reason was far more bizarre. William Seymour's newsletter, *The Apostolic Faith*, with over fifty thousand subscribers, had ceased publication. Much of the Garr's support in the United States came from those who read their mission updates in Seymour's newsletter. But Seymour had not chosen to end his publication; someone made that decision for him.

His two administrative assistants were furious with Seymour, because he had gotten married. They believed he was compromising and that the Lord would return at any moment and everyone had to be busy doing kingdom business. So they stole his mailing list of subscribers and moved hundreds of miles away. Things were changing for everyone.

Learning to Let Go

Alfred and Lillian soon realized they had returned to a completely different situation than before. First, Mok Lai Chi had emerged into a significant leader; one that Alfred deemed worthy to lead the work there. Second, Alfred's calling was becoming more refined in his own mind. He realized that his calling was to plant and not to pastor. He reveals this in his own words.

> *As the Lord has put evangelistic work upon myself and my wife, we can not tell how long we will remain in China…*
>
> *We are working to get them (Chinese) established as much as possible, and we are seeing fruit…Brother Mok is the head of the work here…*

Alfred continued in that letter by asking people to support Mok Lai Chi financially. He soon realized it would be difficult for Brother Mok to become an assistant or translator again, after leading the Mission for almost two years. Alfred focused on establishing the Missionary Home and doing evangelistic work.

While they were pondering how they should move forward, they began receiving requests to return to India. After praying about these invitations, they received an urgent request from Maud Orelebar, who had a significant missionary work in Bombay. They decided it was time to go.

Back to India

With Mok Lai Chi already in charge of the Mission, Alfred and Lillian only had to turn over the Missionary Home to someone. They decided that Brother McIntosh could handle this part of the ministry and gave it into his care. They left for India in late January and arrived in Bombay in early February 1910. They started working immediately.

Alfred Garr in India

During this trip, they labored both among the English and Native speaking people. They held meetings throughout central and northern India over the next four months. These meetings drew large crowds of both unbelievers and Christians seeking to be baptized in the Holy Spirit. These were possibly their most powerful meetings to date.

Although their meetings were powerful, few stories are relevant except two. First, many of the believers who attended their meetings, seeking the baptism of the Holy Spirit, were those who had opposed and persecuted them on their previous trip. Now God had turned the persecutors into seekers.

Second, in July Lillian began to suffer terribly from the heat which was substantially worse than usual that summer. The immediate reports said she suffered with a serious fever at this time, but another reason was soon found for her sensitivity. Lillian was pregnant.

Back to Hong Kong

Although they were phenomenally successful in India, they began feeling the Lord directing them to leave. They were not quite sure where to go, but they realized the Lord was directing them. Alfred and Lillian, now pregnant, returned to Hong Kong in autumn 1910.

Joseph King, already on his around the world trip, joined them in Hong Kong in December. His teaching ministry among the believers was powerful. Alfred and Lillian requested he stay and begin a Bible school in Hong Kong, until he reminded them that he had received a world-wide commission, which they quickly remembered.

Alfred was soon re-engaged in establishing the Missionary Home. Brother McIntosh had decided to close it down in his absence. McIntosh believed that it was too expensive and cost prohibitive to keep open. Alfred, on the other hand, was sure that it must remain open, regardless of the financial costs.

Finances were a difficult issue for many missionaries during this time and this was one reason behind Alfred's desire to open this home. He had faith for finances and wanted to use that gift to serve others, while they, in turn, served the Lord.

Abased and Abounding

Alfred and Lillian were not coddled Americans living a life of ease and comfort on the mission field. They were tough missionaries, sacrificing their lives, actually laying them down, for the Lord and the gospel. They often went through times of severe lack in their lives as they sought to obey the Lord.

The concept of need and lack was different then and now. Throughout the last few years of ministry, Alfred and Lillian had lived meagerly, focusing on serving God and His people, not themselves. Blanche Appleby, a co-worker with Alfred and Lillian, provides this testimony of their meal schedule in Hong Kong.

> *The days that followed were days of...testings, chiefly financial testings. We had only two meals daily, consisting of rice, poverty gravy (grease, flour & water)...*
>
> *Occasionally Pentecostal gravy (which had small bits of meat in it), now and then one egg each, and a special treat was hot biscuits, rarely enjoyed.*
>
> *We had beans, perhaps a few times weekly and sometimes curry. Our portions were skimpy and we felt very empty, especially prior to 10 a.m. and 4 p.m.*

The Garrs and other early Pentecostal missionaries paid a price for their service to the Lord. John G. Lake would lose his wife on the mission field in South Africa in 1912, because of sickness brought on by malnutrition. Alfred and Lillian had already paid a dear price as well, but God had honored their faith and sacrifice.

A Son Is Born

In spring 1911, the Lord brought joy into their lives. In the land where they had sown two daughters and a faithful co-worker over three years before, God gave them a son.

Alfred Gaeleton Garr, Jr. was born by caesarian section on April 9, 1911. The doctors said there was no way Lillian would live through the childbirth or operation. But she did.

Alfred and Lillian Garr, with son, Alfred Jr., 1913

Although it was a difficult time for them, according to Alfred's testimony, God miraculously worked out problem after problem.

One pressing problem was feeding their new son. Accounts differ, but either Lillian did not have enough milk due to her own health crisis, or the baby could not tolerate her milk. Either way it was a significant and looming problem. Alfred did what he always did in times of crisis—he prayed.

While praying and crying out to God to spare his son's life, he heard these four words, "Eagle Brand Condensed Milk." He rose up immediately from prayer and began searching for a store that sold this product, but could find none.

At the last store he visited, the owner looked shocked when Alfred made his request for condensed milk. The owner said he had never heard of this type of milk before, but that a box of cans had arrived recently, though he had not ordered them. When he retrieved them from his shelves it turned out to be Eagle Brand Condensed Milk. Alfred, Jr. survived on that milk until Lillian was sufficiently recovered.

Redeeming the Time

Within months, it was time for the Garrs to return to North America. The Mission was well established by this time and they left Hong Kong dramatically different than before. Although their last trip was very successful, they had left for the United States in sorrow.

Now things were different. In India, those who had persecuted them before, now received them. Where their prophetic word to Dr. King had been rejected in the States, they saw it fulfilled in Hong Kong. Where they had buried their daughters years before, now they were bringing home a son. With victory swallowing up the memory of their hardships before, the Garrs left Hong Kong to return to North America.

CHAPTER EIGHT

INTO THE FRAY

Over the last six years, Alfred and Lillian had taken God at His word and found Him faithful. He had sent them around the world twice to preach the gospel, plant churches, and make disciples. He had given them success in each place. Now they returned to North America for a new assignment.

They traveled throughout California in 1912, briefly pastoring a mission congregation in Los Angeles. For the next year they traveled mostly on the West Coast speaking at conventions. Alfred then departed for six months to India, Arabia, and Persia. When he returned to the States, they settled in Los Angeles because of difficulties that were surfacing in the Pentecostal movement at that time. Although this has no bearing on his story, it was during this time that Alfred also legally changed both he and his son's middle name from Gaeleton to Goodrich.

The Divisions Begin

The Azusa Street revival had accomplished some amazing things. The truth of the baptism in the Holy Spirit and the power it brought was recovered for the church. For many believers the "color-line" was erased from the church as blacks and whites worshiped and ministered together more freely. Also, sectarianism due to doctrinal differences had been confronted and dealt with for many believers.

But in 1914, approximately eight years later, trouble was brewing in the Pentecostal movement. Divisions had reformed underneath the surface—some along racial lines and others emerged from doctrinal disagreements. Others were simply personality clashes that were seeking more spiritual sounding reasons to separate.

The doctrinal differences that emerged were varied. Some Pentecostal leaders taught that speaking in tongues was the initial evidence of the baptism of the Holy Spirit. Others believed that love and the removal of sectarianism was the real sign. The latter group was especially concerned that the primacy of tongues might bring more division and disunity.

The New Issues

Two other doctrinal issues arose which shook the movement. The first was the emergence of the "Finished Work Pentecostals." As opposed to the "Holiness Pentecostals," they did not believe in a separate and distinct experience of sanctification. They taught that believers were sanctified positionally at the New Birth and grew into holiness experientially as they walked in obedience to God.

The second issue was the "Oneness Doctrine." Some leaders developed this teaching to replace the doctrine of the Trinity. They taught that there was only one God, who revealed Himself completely in Jesus. They rejected the co-existence of the Father, Son, and Holy Spirit as the Trinitarians taught. They taught a person had to be baptized in the name of Jesus to be saved. They believed a baptism in the name of the Father, Son, and Holy Spirit was invalid.

Into the Fray

This was the environment that Alfred Garr soon found himself in. Los Angeles had been distinguished as the center of the Pentecostal awakening in North America. Now it emerged as the center of Pentecostal divisions as well.

From his Burning Bush days, Alfred had seen how quickly divisions could emerge over the smallest issues. They had used any point of contention as a reason to denounce and separate from each other. Now the Pentecostal movement, born of the revival which had delivered him from this kind of sectarianism, was threatening to split apart.

When he arrived back in the United States, Alfred settled in Los Angeles, and sought help with the debates which were raging between the different groups. In early 1914, Alfred rented a large warehouse type building and planted a congregation he called The Garage.

Alfred embraced the "Finished Work Doctrine," although he had been powerfully impacted by the Holiness message. He believed that holiness was possible *and* necessary, but he was beginning to see that holiness was appropriated by faith in what Jesus had accomplished (the finished work) not by human works. He did not reject the standards of holiness, just the Holiness movement's method of obtaining it.

He had seen many that supposedly found holiness through their own seeking or works only to become very unholy in their attitudes and actions. Alfred had personal experience that knowledge puffs up and human striving produces bitterness. This was the error that had reduced the Burning Bush from a powerful movement toward becoming a legalistic, controlling sect.

Speaking the Truth in Love

Alfred could have never been considered a compromiser. He stood for the truth regardless of the personal cost. But when he stood in the middle of the "Finished Work debate," he fought for the doctrine which he believed in strongly, but he also fought for unity. He and others were successful in keeping the unity of the spirit in the bond of peace, for a season, while this debate continued.

The Oneness issue was a little different, because it threatened to divide the Pentecostal movement more quickly and deeply and there appeared to be little merit to this new doctrine. It seemed to merely be a point of contention over theoretical concepts, but one which produced no fruit other than division.

The division was not just over the concept of the Godhead, but over baptism. The Oneness movement began teaching that the correct formula required baptism in Jesus' name. Some began to teach that anyone not baptized according to the correct formula was not really saved.

In response, Alfred wrote a scathing denunciation of this doctrine in a widely read Pentecostal publication. It was sarcastically entitled, *"Have you been baptized in the name of Jesus?"* Alfred ridiculed the idea of being baptized in the name of Jesus as being necessary for salvation.

Remarkably, although he denounced the doctrine, he continued to fellowship with those who promoted it. Frank Ewart, the leader of the Oneness movement, was a close friend and they maintained their friendship through this conflict. They even continued ministering together for a while, but Alfred restricted Ewart from preaching this doctrine when they did.

Opening a Well

While working to help unify the Pentecostals, Alfred joined the newly formed Assemblies of God, even though he did not embrace some of their philosophical points, such as not ordaining women and their belief in separation of the races.

The Assemblies quickly became the most popular and widespread Pentecostal group. Alfred was instantly influential in their denomination and was a featured speaker at their main convention in Chicago in September, 1914.

Alfred continued to be concerned about the direction the Pentecostal movement was headed, but soon realized he could not turn the tide without supernatural intervention. He began focusing his time and energies on reviving the movement, instead of simply trying to correct wrong doctrines with good teaching.

He decided to bring a number of nationally known evangelists and "new talent" to The Garage for special meetings in an effort to re-ignite the Pentecostal Movement on the West Coast. This turned into a powerful time of revival beginning in late 1914. Two well known ministers of that time provide their perspective on these meetings.

I had an opportunity to visit the great revival in LA in 1914. Dr. Garr, by faith, rented a huge building and brought to LA many of the great preachers of that day...This was one of the greatest revivals ever conducted in that part of the country.
—Clarence Erickson

He rented a garage building, which would seat about two thousand...From that meeting, there seemed to emanate a new faith, a new zeal, a new power...There was no issue, no dogma, and no eccentric message of any kind...
—William Opie

These meetings did not focus on correcting the "new issues;" they sought to reawaken the hunger for God that had marked the birth of the Pentecostal movement. According to William Opie, many people found "a new faith, a new zeal, a new power" during this time. God was moving again in Los Angeles.

In retrospect, like most before them, the Pentecostal movement had begun infighting for one main reason—they had stopped moving. When their forward progress had slowed, they began arguing and dividing over different doctrines. Alfred had found the way to change a movement that was headed in the wrong direction—get it moving again.

The Next Level

God was blessing Alfred's ministry, but he was not content. He longed for a deeper experience in God for himself and the movement. He desired to see the raw power of God released to propel them even further. To facilitate this, he invited Maria Woodworth-Etter to come to The Garage for an extended series of meetings.

Maria Woodworth-Etter's ministry had been distinguished by signs and wonders for fifteen years *prior* to the Azusa Street Outpouring. She had traveled across America for more than thirty years in a powerful evangelistic and revival ministry. She began ministering at

The Garage, on October 4, 1915, and God moved powerfully. Alfred reports on her ministry there.

> *Tumors, cancers, fevers, lameness, deafness, blindness, and many other things produced by the Enemy have yielded to the "prayer of faith," and the results are faith inspiring indeed. One sister who was prayed over was relieved of a tumor that weighed one pound and three quarter, and had eight roots.*

These meetings were widely attended by people from all over America, not just California. There was a visible glory that manifested over the crowd several times. In addition to the healings and miracles which occurred, a number of people also began having visions and angelic visitations. The movement in Los Angeles was beginning to blaze again.

Because of the impact Alfred was having on the West Coast, he was elected as an Executive Presbyter of the Assemblies of God in October, 1915. This was their international board of overseers comprised of twelve ministers. Alfred was elected in absentia, because he was too busy in these meetings to attend the convention.

A Severe Test

Alfred Garr had found great success and was poised for advancement. He was recognized as an international leader of the Pentecostal movement. His congregation in Los Angeles was moving in power on the West Coast and helping lead the Pentecostals back to their first love. But a severe test was coming.

Near the end of 1915, Lillian became sick. Her illness progressed into the early part of 1916, until it became serious. As her sickness continued growing steadily worse, suddenly Alfred also became ill. Near the end of February 1916, both of them were bedridden.

For the past fifteen years of their marriage, Alfred and Lillian Garr had been a powerful team in ministry. They had traveled the world together, preaching and ministering. They had borne three children together and planted two in the soil of the Orient as "seeds of the gospel."

The nature of Lillian's illness is not recorded, but it continued until April. Finally after being advised that only surgery could save her life, Alfred and Lillian consented. She died at the age of thirty-eight on April 12, 1916 as a result of complications from the surgery. Alfred Garr was devastated.

Coming Back Together

Lillian had been a wonderful Bible teacher, but really much more than that. She had possessed a profound and open heart for the lost and for the body of Christ at large. Twelve hundred people attended her memorial service. Alfred said at her funeral, although some people had different opinions about him, everyone loved his wife.

Lillian was so loved that all of the differing factions of Pentecostal Christianity came together for her memorial service. Oneness, Trinitarians, Holiness, and Finished Work Pentecostals were all there. They dropped their differences to carry her casket.

Her pallbearers were a virtual "Who's Who" of the movement, including most of the American leaders and Canadian leaders. Alfred was so sick that he had to be pushed in a wheelchair to the graveside service. Stanley Frodsham writes about Lillian's influence in the movement.

> *It would be difficult to find one more universally loved in Pentecostal circles, and I believe I express the sentiments of all who have ever heard her when I write that we have lost the most spiritual teacher we had from our ranks...She always had something fresh from God...*
>
> *There must have been quite twelve hundred of the saints at the funeral yesterday, and it was good to find the Pentecostal people of*

> *Los Angeles were really all one in heart, despite doctrinal differences...*
>
> *At her funeral all the Pentecostal saints of Los Angeles, who have been divided by various doctrinal dissensions, were all melted together into one. John 17 seemed to be fulfilled in Los Angeles yesterday as we laid dear Sister Garr to her last resting place.*

Lillian's death and memorial service was an important milestone for the entire Pentecostal movement. From Lillian's memorial service, a cry began to come forth calling for love to triumph over the doctrinal differences that had divided the movement.

The Last Straw

Lillian's death and his own sickness were also a turning point in Alfred's life. In his despair over her death and his weakness from his own sickness, Alfred was broken and sought God on a new level. He was convicted by the Lord during this time that he still lacked perfect love.

Although he had grown in love and was trying to maintain unity with others, he was still prone to anger and judgment in his heart. He could also still be quite caustic in his writings. He began to seek God for a cleansing of his heart and a baptism of purer love. He went through a profound time of brokenness as God revealed the hardness which remained in his heart.

Alfred's health deteriorated further and the diagnosis was bad—stomach cancer. He was bedridden and unable to eat solid food for months. He became thinner, weaker, and sicker daily. He stayed in the home of a Baptist pastor and this gentleman's wife cared for Alfred and his young son, Alfred, Jr.

One day while lying in bed, almost too weak to think, Alfred began to pray. He told the Lord that he had been prepared for evangelism and revival, and that his death would serve no great purpose. As he prayed, Alfred realized if Jesus were on the earth that day, he could go to Him and be healed. He then realized that Jesus was there in his room—not physically, but by His Spirit.

Alfred realized that he could be healed by Jesus right there. So he rolled over in his bed and weakly got on his knees. He prayed and declared, *"Lord I believe You will heal me now."* Alfred said that he felt like oil flowed all over his body and penetrated him completely. Every last bit of his pain disappeared.

He then prayed, *"God if I am healed, then I going to get up and act like a well man."* He requested that his clothes be brought to him and a large, full meal be prepared. Although the pastor's wife thought he had lost his mind, she complied, figuring it would probably be his last meal.

With phenomenal effort he dressed himself. Even though his pain was gone, he was still weak. He could barely walk so he pushed a chair and shuffled along behind it into the dining room. He sat up with great effort, waiting for the food to arrive.

He ate the entire meal and shuffled back to bed exhausted. He repeated this pattern throughout the next week. The only evidence of his healing was the lack of pain and the ability to eat and hold down solid food. He was still too weak to do anything else on his own and he was still very drawn and sickly looking. However, over the next month, as he continued to proclaim his healing, his strength returned, and he was soon fully recovered.

Healed... But Not Whole

Although Alfred was healed physically, he was still not whole. His other half was with the Lord and he was still a broken man. He was struggling in his soul to find the perfect love he believed was possible to attain. He sought something deeper in God.

He felt the Lord directing him to make some changes. While leading The Garage over the past two years, Lillian had done much of the pastoral and teaching work. After both of their illnesses had started, Alfred added others who helped administrate and teach.

Alfred decided to leave the church in the hands of those he had raised up and return to the evangelistic ministry. He left Los Angeles in early autumn 1916 and traveled with his young son to begin again in a new ministry thrust.

They traveled first to St. Louis, Missouri, for the General Council meeting of the Assemblies of God. As an Executive Presbyter, Alfred was responsible to address the issues facing their denomination. They were gathering at this time to deal with the correct baptismal formula dispute within their denomination.

Alfred sympathized with the Trinitarians, but was bothered about the establishment of a written creed designed in part to control others. The written records from that meeting contain no comments from Alfred on this issue. Either he was silent on the issue or his comments were edited out. Regardless, he preached passionately for two nights in the main evening services which accompanied the General Council meetings.

After these meetings, Alfred resigned his position as an Executive Presbyter of the Assemblies of God and possibly withdrew his ordination as well. From St. Louis he traveled to Kentucky to visit relatives, prior to launching his new evangelistic ministry.

After leaving Kentucky, Alfred, his son, and Billy Black, a noted evangelist, traveled throughout the Midwest, South, and West Coast of America in an itinerant ministry. His ministry during this time was distinguished by hundreds coming to the Lord with some divine healings taking place. Hundreds were also baptized in the Holy Spirit. The crowds were blessed, but Alfred would refer back to this time as a two-year period of discouragement and depression.

An Important Lesson

In February 1918, Alfred and Billy Black arrived in Dallas, Texas, to hold meetings at F.F. Bosworth's church. While the meetings were in progress, Bosworth asked Alfred and Billy Black to oversee his congregation while he traveled for a few months. They agreed.

Alfred was not impressed by the state of the congregation and the direction it was headed. After Bosworth left, Alfred found dissension in the congregation about the issue of tongues as being a necessary evidence of the Holy Spirit baptism. He also felt there was a lack of zeal and passion among the congregation.

His first sermon as an overseer of the congregation in Bosworth's absence deepened the divide. He preached what some called "the best sermon on the baptism with the Holy Spirit and the initial evidence" they had ever heard—before or since. It galvanized the spiritually hungry among the congregation, but somewhat ostracized another group within.

But soon the meetings were heralded as a kind of revival by *The Weekly Evangel*, an influential Pentecostal magazine. Letters and reports came out which were highly supportive of Alfred's ministry at the congregation. Within weeks, the elders of the congregation wrote a letter to the Assemblies of God implying that Bosworth should no longer be their pastor.

In response F.F. Bosworth wrote a letter to the Assemblies of God, implicating Alfred as the source of the letter. He was obviously hurt and felt betrayed by the letter and by Alfred. Bosworth resigned as pastor of the congregation in April 1918 and from the Assemblies of God three months later. He would go on to become one of the foremost healing evangelists of the twentieth century.

Although Alfred did not realize it at the time, this episode would provide him with one of his most important lessons for the remainder of his life and ministry. It would help direct some of the most powerful ministry he would have over the next two decades. This lesson is addressed in the next chapter and is also an interesting aspect of apostolic ministers.

A New Beginning

Alfred left Billy Black with the Dallas congregation in early May to briefly fulfill a previous commitment in Los Angeles. He joined a series of powerful meetings which were already in process. He had agreed to bring messages specifically designed to impart a burden and vision for missions at this convention.

Hannah Garr

While ministering at this gathering, Alfred reconnected with R.L. Erickson and family, who were living near Los Angeles. Erickson had been a longtime friend, dating back to the Burning Bush days. Alfred began courting Erickson's daughter, Hannah, and they were married several months later on July 26, 1918.

His choice of Hannah as a bride caused a "bit of a stir" in Pentecostal circles because of their age difference. Alfred was forty-four and Hannah was twenty-two. Also, his friends in Los Angeles had already decided that Alfred should marry a particular lady evangelist. Alfred apparently did not agree.

Alfred had not married Hannah because of her age or looks, although she was beautiful. He married her because the Lord had shown him that Hannah would have the same mantle and anointing of prayer that her mother had. Her mother had been a powerful prayer warrior, and Hannah would eventually follow in those footsteps, as will be seen.

After a short honeymoon, Alfred and Hannah traveled back to Dallas, Texas to resume co-pastoring with Billy Black. The congregation in Dallas was not overjoyed at Alfred's choice of a wife either. They also felt that God had spoken to them concerning a bride for Alfred among their own congregation. But Alfred had made the right choice.

Hannah was so gracious that everyone was soon won over. Over time she became a leading figure in the Pentecostal movement nationally. She also became a wonderful stepmother to Alfred's son, Alfred, Jr. Her own mother had died when she was still young and her relationship with her stepmother was less than good. Hannah understood issues involved with step parenting and did not make the same mistakes.

In the spring of 1919, Alfred turned the congregation in Dallas over to two others and moved his family to the Los Angeles area. They would base their ministry there for the next decade as they traveled across America holding a remarkable series of meetings and birthing literally hundreds of churches. The secular newspapers would proclaim the healings, miracles, and salvations which occurred through his ministry during those days of revival.

CHAPTER NINE

APOSTOLIC ASPECTS

Although some of Alfred Garr's most significant ministry was still ahead of him, this juncture provides a good opportunity to examine the apostolic aspects of his ministry. Some of these traits have been mentioned throughout the narrative, but require a little more explanation here.

There is quite a bit of discussion currently about apostles and their function in the modern church. Some of the ideas put forth are good, however others are not exactly biblical. Many of them are based more on twenty-first century ideas of success and western leadership than a biblical examination of apostolic function and ministry.

We need greater understanding of this ministry in order to integrate it into church and kingdom life. However, if we try to implement well-intentioned but inaccurate ideas about this ministry, we may cause more damage than the good we intend. We need a biblical understanding of the apostolic ministry to move forward in this endeavor.

Alfred Garr was a modern twentieth century apostle. His life is an illustration of the biblical aspects of this ministry. By examining his life in light of these principles, our understanding of the apostolic ministry and function can be greatly illuminated.

Contradictions

Alfred's ministry was inspiring and impacting, but often controversial and sometimes contradictory. He was aggressive and confrontational, yet he fought for love and unity at the same time. He was forceful enough to enter uncharted territories and stake a claim for the kingdom of God. Yet he would humble himself quickly when needed and change whenever he saw he was wrong.

He fired his mentor, W.E. Shepard and took over his congregation, but then yielded it to another man, at God's direction within months. He fought for unity in the Pentecostal movement and then split F.F. Bosworth's congregation the next year. In each case, he believed he was following God's will. These "contradictions" may bother us, but they are often seen in the Bible in those called to apostolic ministries.

Paul was a contradictory man as well—from the human perspective. He would aggressively fight to keep the message of grace he preached unpolluted. But he would also take a Jewish vow, according to the law, to help heal the division between Jewish and Gentile believers (see Acts 21:24).

Everyone would love to have perfect leaders, but they really do not exist. Leaders (or anyone else for that matter) seldom do anything perfectly, but the main point is *they do something*. Leaders make a way where there was no way before. They shake things up in a good way. They move us forward and this often requires a vision which appears unreasonable and a persistence that can be mistaken for stubbornness.

Leadership is a key element of the apostolic ministry and we desperately need it today. Without leaders we will simply maintain the status quo or even go backwards. Alfred Garr was a forceful man—one who could get things accomplished. He was strong willed and struggled at times with anger and stubbornness, but this appears to be common for apostolic leaders.

Angry Men

Anger and stubbornness are not apostolic traits, but they do seem to be traits often of those whom God calls as apostles. God does not make people angry so they can be apostolic, but he seemingly calls people with great capacities for anger into this ministry.

Paul had been an angry man—he was a murderer and a persecutor of the church. However, his anger propelled him to accomplishment.

James and John had serious issues with anger as well. They wanted to use the power which Jesus had given them for healing and blessing, to kill people instead (see Luke 9:54). We may not appreciate it, but these three men were each chosen by God for apostolic ministry.

Alfred Garr also had a high capacity for anger. And like each of these apostolic men before him, Alfred went through deep dealings of God. Because, though God often calls those with great capacities for anger into this ministry, **"the wrath of man does not produce the righteousness of God" (James 1:20).**

Alfred dealt with anger off and on throughout his ministry. His passion and zeal for God caused conflicts a number of times. But the fire that burned in his soul was necessary for the fulfillment of his ministry. A man of a less forceful spirit could not have endured or accomplished what Alfred did.

Other biblical apostles also struggled with anger during their ministries. Paul and Barnabas had argued over John Mark's inclusion on a venture so strongly that they separated (see Acts 15:39). Peter and Paul had a loud public disagreement (see Galatians 2:14) over key issues of grace. Those God calls to apostolic ministry are generally strong-willed, and they are definitely not weak.

Our modern ideas of what an apostle looks like and what distinguishes their ministry are in significant need of adjustment. We need the ministry of apostles, so we must be able to recognize one in our midst. Alfred Garr was a twentieth century apostle based on the New Testament criterion, and a quick review of his ministry can aid our quest.

Consider these apostolic elements of his ministry:

1) Being Sent By God

The literal meaning of the word apostle is *sent one*. God had sent Alfred to over twelve nations preaching the gospel with remarkable success. In addition to India, Hong Kong, China, and Japan, Alfred had traveled to Sri Lanka, Tibet, Arabia, Persia, Egypt, Palestine, Sumatra, Indonesia, and Malaysia. Mission organizations years later would single out Alfred's ministry as uniquely effective.

Because he was sent by God, Alfred's timing was often divinely impeccable. He stepped into the right situations at the right time and had maximum impact because of it. Although some of his contemporaries thought he was simply restless, the fruit of his ministry testified that his travels were initiated by God.

2) Signs, Wonders, and Mighty Deeds

Signs, wonders, and mighty deeds follow apostles (see II Corinthians 12:12). Alfred's ministry was marked by supernatural signs and wonders. Physical healings, miraculous provision, and even creative miracles occurred in his ministry.

Alfred had other signs and wonders follow his ministry. In the early days, when he was a Burning Bush evangelist, his meetings were known for the deep conviction of sin that gripped people, causing them to publicly confess their sins. This was a wonder.

Later, people were baptized in the Holy Spirit wherever he ministered. Some of these had tarried for "the baptism" for years, but they quickly received in Alfred's meetings, often to the amazement of their pastors. This was also a sign. Alfred also did mighty deeds such as pioneering the gospel in foreign nations and birthing hundreds of churches.

3) Being Displayed as a Spectacle

Paul wrote this about apostles in I Corinthians 4:9:

> **...I think that God hath set forth us the apostles last, as it were appointed to death: for we are made a spectacle unto the world, and to angels, and to men.**

Alfred's ministry was often so radical that it demanded attention which in turn brought persecution, public ridicule, and much misunderstanding. By blazing new trails, Alfred's ministry drew a lot of attention.

From his Burning Bush time to the last days of his life, the secular newspapers would continually report on his meetings, without him requesting it. God would then use this notoriety to promote the gospel to those who would never have attended a church meeting. But many came to the Lord as a result. Like Paul, Alfred caused a stir wherever he went.

4) Persecution and Suffering

Unfortunately, persecution and suffering are part of the apostolic calling as well. Paul was promised suffering from the initial days of his salvation (see Acts 9:16). Jesus' other apostles were promised suffering for their ministries as well (see Matthew 20:23). Alfred Garr also received the cup of suffering.

Persecution, misunderstanding, and rumors followed him throughout his ministry. In India he was the subject of rumors from the moment he set foot in the country. Once meetings began there, other pastors would sometimes enter the building and interrupt Alfred as he ministered, trying to remove their congregants from the service.

In Hong Kong, the criminal element tried to keep the meetings from happening. The police had to be called in to restrain them from harassing and attacking the people who were trying to enter the building. The level of written persecution and slander that arose from their first mission ventures would be akin to someone filling Christian websites with slander and false rumors today.

Additionally, he and Lillian endured hunger, periods of forced fasting, and seasons of lack as a result of their service to God. They did all of this to help people who would probably never understand or appreciate their ministry and calling.

5) Death Works Life

Paul had this written about his apostolic ministry:

> **But we have this treasure in earthen vessels, that the excellency of the power may be of God, and not of us.**
>
> **We are troubled on every side, yet not distressed; we are perplexed, but not in despair;**
>
> **Persecuted, but not forsaken; cast down, but not destroyed;**
>
> **Always bearing about in the body the dying of the Lord Jesus, that the life also of Jesus might be made manifest in our body.**
>
> **For we which live are always delivered unto death for Jesus; sake, that the life also of Jesus might be made manifest in our mortal flesh.**
>
> **So then death works in us, but life in you (II Corinthians 4:7-12)**

Apostles' lives often appear somewhat tragic. They are surrounded by difficulty, persecution, and distress, but God uses this to release His life through them, to other people. Paul repeatedly wrote about the difficulty he endured to fulfill his ministry.

Judge Nothing Now

Much of the emphasis on modern apostles appears to be based on visible success. How many churches are connected to them? How big the churches are, etc. But a closer reading of the Bible reveals that we should not judge anything prior to the right time. In I Corinthians 4, Paul writes:

> **Let a man so account of us, as of the ministers of Christ, and stewards of the mysteries of God.**
>
> **Moreover it is required in stewards, that a man be found faithful.**

But with me it is a very small thing that I should be judged of you, or of man's judgment: yea, I judge not mine own self.

For I know nothing by myself; yet am I not hereby justified: but he that judgeth me is the Lord.

Therefore judge nothing before the time, until the Lord come... (I Corinthians 4:1-5).

Apostle's lives and ministries may not appear to be singularly successful. Consider that by 1919, Alfred had labored for close to twenty years, preaching the gospel—sacrificing his life and family to serve the Lord. What did he have to show for it—a large congregation with loving devotees or acclaim from many different branches of the church world? No—in human terms he had very little to show for his years of sacrifice.

The Burning Bush, to which he had devoted almost five years of his life, had moved further into legalism and control. The Azusa Street Mission was long gone, and many of his Pentecostal friends and co-workers were squabbling and fighting over small differences in doctrine.

The Pentecostal denominations that had been formed appeared to be headed toward political control and exclusivity. Had he devoted his life to this? Had he lost two children and a wife for this? At this point, Alfred Garr was more like Paul, the apostle, than we may realize at first glance.

We hold Paul in high esteem and we celebrate his life, but do we really consider his life? He suffered tremendously for the gospel he preached. He was constantly persecuted and worried about the legalistic teachers who followed him, infecting the new churches with their leaven.

Near the end of his life, he appeared to be a complete failure. Paul was in prison, most of his friends had abandoned him, and the churches he had planted were headed toward error in spite of his care and warnings. But Paul had fulfilled an apostolic ministry, although he did not appear to be successful according to our modern standards.

As Rick Joyner insightfully pointed out, Paul had probably forgotten about those letters he had written to the churches he planted. It is possible that he never even thought about the impact they might have. But consider how much fruit those few letters have born over the last two thousand years as key components of the New Testament.

What may appear to be failure could actually bring great success. Apostles' lives are often marked by death, difficulty, persecution, misunderstanding, and apparent failure. But from this death—life comes out of them toward others. This is an apostolic function.

6) Freedom and Innovation

Freedom and innovation are also apostolic traits. Paul wrote that he received the gospel by revelation, not by man. He then preached it openly before receiving permission from the other apostles, although he eventually did communicate with them. Peter preached the gospel to the Gentiles at Cornelius' house without receiving permission from the council either.

Alfred was often revolutionary in his approach to ministry as well. When the apostolic languages did not work out in India, he adjusted and also discovered biblically a more thorough understanding of tongues in the believer's life.

Throughout his ministry he tried new approaches to evangelism, using music and drama to attract crowds and then preaching to them. In addition he incorporated divine healing into evangelism before this was popular and instituted reforms in worship in the Pentecostal movement. William Opie reported on this:

> *For the first time in Pentecost we began to play musical instruments; for the first time a man actually sang a solo!*

Many of the saints at that time thought it would grieve the Holy Spirit, but Dr. Garr said, "Anything that glorifies Christ will never grieve the Holy Spirit."

Alfred, like other apostolic ministers, was creative and innovative in his approach to ministry as will be seen in the next chapter. He also possessed the freedom to try these new approaches before they were popular. These are small examples, but this is an important biblical attribute of apostles.

7) Establishing Churches

Apostles are called to plant and establish churches. When defending his apostleship, Paul pointed to the Corinthian church and said that they were proof of his apostolic calling and ministry (see I Corinthians 9:2).

Alfred planted congregations in the United States and foreign nations, although he seldom pastored them much beyond their inception. Other leaders, who took over these congregations, often appeared more successful than Alfred because he seldom stuck around to enjoy success. He generally left to plant other churches.

Some modern definitions hold that an apostle is one who leads a large church or organizes existing churches into a larger grouping of connected churches. This may be an apostolic function, but the apostolic ministry mentioned biblically appears to be mostly opposite to the idea.

The biblical pattern is similar to what Alfred functioned in. Paul established congregations and released them to others for pastoral ministry. This freed him to continue moving forward in church planting ministry, ideally with the established churches partnering in faith, finances, and other support.

The calling of an apostle appears to be more about starting and releasing churches, rather than gathering and maintaining them.

8) Not Building on Another's Foundation

This aspect appears to be true of some apostles, but not all. Paul said that he did not want to build on another man's foundation (see Romans 15:20). Paul did not mean that he would not help others with their labors. He meant that his calling was to establish churches from ground zero. He was a foundation layer. Alfred had this same calling.

Throughout his ministry, whenever Alfred had gone to an existing work, he seldom had great success. His ministry was to begin something from scratch—to lay the foundations. He had done this in Hong Kong very successfully; but when he returned the second time, there apparently was tension between him and Mok Lai Chi.

However, when Alfred realized that Mok was supposed to be in charge now, Alfred labored in evangelism instead of trying to take back the leadership. Then things worked. Alfred had planted and Mok was watering, but upon returning Alfred had difficulty finding a place to fit.

When Alfred had pastored the existing mission congregation in Los Angeles in 1912, he did okay. However, when he planted The Garage less than two years later, it was wildly successful. When Alfred traveled during 1916 to 1918, he was struggling with depression and heaviness in his soul. Some was no doubt from the death of his wife, but there was another reason.

During this time, he held evangelistic meetings in established churches and missions and they were successful, but he was unfulfilled. Then when he took over Bosworth's congregation in Dallas, he was very unhappy with the foundation he found, so he re-laid it. Bosworth was offended and resigned from the congregation and denomination as a result.

All of this occurred because Alfred was not called to build on another man's foundation—he was called to lay foundations. When he saw another's foundation (Bosworth's), he was not happy with it and uprooted it, so he could lay his own. This was a result of his calling and gift, not an inability to work with others. He had already proven his ability to function in a team, even with those he disagreed with strongly.

To balance this concept, there are those with apostolic callings such as Apollos who are called to water where others plant (see I Corinthians 3:6). He was apparently an excellent teacher, who could build wonderfully on another man's foundation, but this was not Paul or Alfred's ministry.

Conclusion

We need apostles and their ministry in today's church and world. However, we do not need to embrace blindly everything that is called apostolic. Jesus commended the church at Ephesus, because they judged those who called themselves apostles and were not. We need this same discernment in order to recognize and embrace true apostolic ministry.

Apostolic ministry will bring about change in the church and the world around us. True apostles will birth new moves and movements, and will confront the lukewarmness in the church—not just through their words, but through their lives and ministries. And this was what Alfred Garr did.

As his ministry continued over time, Alfred found greater understanding of some of these principles and became much more fruitful for the kingdom of God. The same will be true of us as well. As we discover the mandates and signs of apostolic ministry and embrace those whom God sends, the church in our generation will find greater fruitfulness and power.

CHAPTER TEN

APOSTLE IN THE UNITED STATES

After settling his family in Los Angeles in the summer of 1919, Alfred assessed his last few years of ministry. He had been fairly successful on the road, but he realized that by ministering in churches he was not reaching the lost effectively. Although hundreds had met the Lord during his eighteen months of traveling, Alfred was ready to see them come to God by the thousands.

In 1920, he decided to try an innovative approach—he went to where the lost were. He and Hannah started a series of daytime meetings at a theater in downtown Los Angeles. They did not rent the entire building and convert it into a church. That would have stopped the non-church traffic, which they wanted to access. The theater continued hosting events in the evening, but the Garrs used the lobby during the day.

Alfred played four musical instruments—the trombone, saxophone, violin, and guitar. Hannah played the piano. They would use their musical talents to draw people to their services in the lobby, then preach the gospel to them. William Ward gives the report:

> *Without funds, but by faith, A.G. Garr rented the Lyceum Theater in Los Angeles for noonday services. Every day at noon for six months, A.G. played his trombone and Mrs. Garr played the piano. Thousands of souls were saved in that Theater during those days.*

Alfred's success in evangelism dramatically increased by going where the lost people were. He went from hundreds meeting the Lord in a year's worth of traveling around the country, to thousands meeting the Lord in six months. During this decade he would seldom hold evangelistic crusades in churches again unless he felt sure the lost would come.

Alfred was convinced in his heart that his ministry was to be a pioneer evangelist. Today, some would call this an apostolic ministry. He now felt called to go, not so much to the churches, but to the world and bring them into the church. After learning some important lessons during his six months at the Lyceum Theatre, Alfred was ready to go into the harvest fields of America.

An Intense Battle

Before he could, however, a crisis arose. In the springtime of 1921, Alfred became sick again and was bedridden for three months. His symptoms were very similar to the episode five years earlier. Once again, he could not eat and it appeared he would not survive. Some of his friends believed it was the end for Alfred.

While he was declining quickly, William Opie contacted Alfred with a Word from God—Alfred was supposed to lead revival meetings in Fresno, California for a month. Not knowing he was sick, Opie requested that Alfred come to Fresno and lead these meetings.

When Opie discovered that Alfred was deathly ill, he was puzzled as to why God would give him this Word. But Alfred took this as the Lord's way of telling him he would not die, but be healed by the time these meetings were scheduled to begin.

So Alfred agreed to lead the meetings, although he was in no shape to do them. Still too sick to walk or do much else, Alfred had Hannah placed a cot in a storage room in their home. She would help him get to the storage room daily, so he could lie on the cot and pray for God to enable him to conduct the meetings.

When the time arrived, Alfred was still too weak to drive, so Hannah drove him to Fresno. He kept telling her along the way, "God is healing me. I will regain my strength in Fresno." She hoped so, because they were expecting him to preach for a full month. He was still unable to eat any solid food when they arrived in Fresno.

This is the Victory—Our Faith

At the beginning of the first meeting, Alfred needed to be helped to the platform, still weak from his sickness. But when he began to preach, he came alive and preached with power, feeling no weakness at all. When he was done, he was exhausted again and too weak to walk without assistance.

Each time he preached he felt a little better after the meeting. Over the course of that month he completely regained his strength and was able to eat whatever he wanted again. He was healed by taking God at His Word and acting on it in faith, without feeling anything at all. But the process of standing in faith for his own healing, released something else—divine healings and miracles on a completely different level.

Divine healing, which up until now had been happening to a small degree, suddenly became prominent in the Fresno meetings. Several healings here were notable. Interestingly enough, Alfred rarely felt any tangible anointing when praying for the sick. He simply prayed in faith and God moved.

He preached in Fresno every night for thirty nights straight and the town was stirred with a powerful revival with hundreds saved. As a result of those meetings, Alfred received requests from all over the West Coast to conduct revival meetings.

A Typical Crusade

After the Fresno meetings, Alfred and Hannah traveled throughout the West Coast region and eventually the Southeastern United States, holding evangelistic campaigns over the next eight years. Literally tens of thousands of people came to the Lord and more than one hundred of churches were established through these revival meetings.

Instead of documenting the scores of campaigns they held, we will focus on several specific meetings to draw out the principles that Alfred employed and the success the Lord gave him. The first of these occurred in Bakersfield, California.

Revival baptism service, Bakersfield California

In September 1922, Alfred teamed up with R.L. Erickson, his friend, and Hannah's father, for a series of meetings in Bakersfield. The meetings were not held in a church, but were "open air meetings" in a vacant lot in town. Hannah was pregnant with their first child and would give birth to a daughter they named Evangeline, near the end of the two-month campaign.

As the meetings began, Alfred focused on evangelism. He preached on the righteousness of God and the failure of mankind to meet it. Erickson focused on teaching about the heart of God and His power to save. Although both men were comfortable moving in power ministry, they did not focus on divine healing during the first weeks of the meetings.

The campaign started off rather slowly, but eventually began to gain momentum, although not much. After almost five weeks of plowing through the indifference and hard-heartedness among the people, Garr and Erickson finally felt they had succeeded at least to a point. There was a core group who were beginning to respond to the call to "get right with God."

Now, Garr and Erickson felt they had a foundation for people to trust God in faith for healing. They quickly announced that they would hold divine healing services and pray for the sick. As soon as they started praying for the sick, a little girl was dramatically healed. Instantly, word spread and the crowds began growing as the curious (and lost) began attending.

Now both God and the evangelists had the people's attention. People began responding to the calls for repentance and flocking to the altars to seek cleansing from their sins. Also as the ministers continued praying for the sick, several additional healings occurred which caused the local newspaper to report on the revival meetings.

BAKERSFIELD, CALIFORNIA, FRIDAY, SEPTEMBER 8, 1922

Healers Create Stir Here
* * *   * * *   * * *   * * *
Faithful Testify to Cures
Throngs Attend Meetings of Revivalists to See Purported Miracles

During the song service which opened the meeting the crowd continued to pour in, until the multitude seated was entirely surrounded by a semi-circle of automobiles and by those who arrived too late to find seats. There was a general stir in the congregation when little Marie Gillespie came in, accompanied by her parents, Mr. and Mrs. S.F. Gillespie, of Riverview. The 7-year old girl has undergone the most sensational of the claimed cures of the evangelists. Besought by friends of the child for prayers for her at the former healing service, the parents of the little girl declare that after suffering for four years from tuberculosis of the spine, which had rendered her entirely helpless for the past 20 months, she was able to rise and walk, even though still encumbered by the plaster cast which has encircled her for so long. Knowing that the child and her parents were to give testimonials at the Thursday night meeting, many Oildale and Riverview people to whom little Marie is well-known, were present...

A newspaper article testifying of God's power to heal was unusual. The 1920s were not a time of religious piety in America. On the contrary, it was a fairly decadent time where entertainment and pleasure were main pursuits. But when crowds gathered because God was healing people at a vacant lot in town through two traveling evangelists, the newspaper reported it.

God was also honoring Alfred's decision to leave the church venues to focus on going to the lost. By doing this, his meetings all started out initially much smaller than if he had stayed within the churches. This created a financial burden for them and also meant that they were responsible to build their own audience for the message. But Alfred saw this as an opportunity to have faith and for the Lord to move powerfully in response.

God did honor Alfred's faith, by releasing saving and healing power to the people. This, in turn, initiated coverage by the newspapers, which provided sensational advertising—much better than he could have purchased. Plus the newspapers lent credibility to the healings by listing names, addresses, and testimonies in print.

As a result, even larger crowds gathered almost immediately. Four days after the first article in the newspaper, the town was so stirred by the revival meetings that another article was published covering the revival that was taking place.

Bakersfield Californian

HUGE CROWD AT HEALING SERVICE

Classes Mingle in Search of Truth; Gillespie Child Still Well:

A monster crowd gathered Monday evening at the revival meeting held in the open air at the corner of Twentieth and M street to investigate at the third divine healing session the truth of miraculous cures claimed for the evangelists, R.L. Erickson and A.G. Garr

...One of the most sensational cures attributed to the evangelists is that of little Marie Gillespie of Oildale. Paralyzed, rendered helpless from an operation, compelled to wear a plaster cast for four years, the child was able to walk after the first prayers of the evangelists, according to the testimonials of her parents. There has been no evidence of a relapse from the first reported cure...the child has now been removed from the plaster cast and is making steady progress in regaining the complete use of her limbs. Not only the poor and lowly, but rich and influential citizens have been attracted to the revival meetings, it was seen at the Monday evening service, when all classes mingled in a spirit of humility.

Remarkably, within two weeks after this second article was published, Alfred felt it was time for him to leave. Although the area was stirred by revival, his job was done. He had come to see sinners cleansed and awakened to faith in God. And God had begun moving in power.

Now it was time for him to move on and pioneer another work in another area. Someone else would have to build on the foundation he had laid. Out of these meetings in Bakersfield, four congregations were formed. Two were planted in Bakersfield, one in Oildale where Marie Gillespie lived, and apparently one more in another suburb. In all, hundreds of people had met the Lord and these new churches could disciple them further and help them grow.

After leaving Bakersfield, Alfred and his family went to Taft, a town about forty miles away, and began meetings there. The miraculous healings, which had begun in Bakersfield continued almost as soon as the meetings in Taft began, and hundreds met the Lord there.

This became a habit with Alfred. When his larger campaigns ended, he would travel to outlying areas on his way to the next major campaign. This enabled him to capitalize on the interest generated from the larger meetings and reap souls from these fields as well.

Over the next five years, Alfred, Hannah, and family held meetings throughout southern and central California, Oregon, Washington, and parts of Canada. In almost every case a church and usually several churches were begun as a direct result of these revivals.

The Pattern of Success

Alfred would generally come into an area, knowing no one or almost no one. He did little or no pre-planning other than prayer and fasting for the people of the area and to prepare his own heart. When he arrived he would locate a place to rent or find a place for a tent or an open-air meeting. He looked for high traffic, high attention areas, having learned the value of going where the people were.

When his meetings began, it was often like plowing through a parking lot. People would be indifferent, hesitant, or many times combative. But Alfred was a strong willed man who was comfortable standing in the storms. He was energized by the challenge, not anxious about it.

Hannah and, eventually, Alfred, Jr. would also help in the meetings. Hannah played the piano during the worship portion of their meetings and would often teach in the afternoon sessions. Alfred, Jr. was gifted with an amazingly beautiful voice and eventually helped with worship time at the beginning of each meeting as well.

In general, Alfred would begin the campaign by preaching pointedly until the people began to move toward God in repentance. He did not attack people, but he did not spare them either. He preached on the righteousness of God and man's failure to live up to it. He stayed squarely on the simple gospel at the beginning of each campaign.

As people came under conviction however, Alfred would seldom lead them in a prayer for salvation. Instead, he invited them to come to the altar and seek God for their own salvation. People would stay at the altar until they had "prayed through" and found cleansing from their sin.

Alfred often told the people in his campaigns, *"If I can convince with my words, someone else can unconvince you. If you get it on your own, no one can take if from you."* When the people found their assurance from God, they did not need to get it from the minister. The people who got saved, stayed saved.

The Power of Spiritual Power

One of Alfred's mottos during this season was: *"Stay until the power falls."* He was committed to continuing any meetings that he began, until the Lord showed up. If Alfred had a difficult first week of meetings, he simply figured he was one week closer to a breakthrough. He would often preach for two or three weeks before any kind of breakthrough came, and sometimes longer.

Many times the breakthrough came because someone was dramatically healed. These healings brought attention to the meetings and brought the curious in; they also heightened people's faith in God. With more people attending and more faith released in the people, a revival atmosphere soon emerged.

Many times entire families would come to the Lord as a result of a power encounter, such as a healing. Any demonstration of power would usually open the hearts of the people. Many times even some of the hardest hearts would melt as God's power was revealed.

In Bakersfield, a lady who was a nominal Catholic came to the meetings and was touched by the Holy Spirit. She gave her life to Jesus as a result. She then took her son, who had a tumor growing in his ear, to the meetings. He got healed and saved. Her husband was awestruck by what God had done for his son, whose condition was so bad he had been scheduled for surgery.

The father attended the meetings, and got saved and healed from a back condition, and was able to return to work full time. Eventually their other son, who was touched by all of this, got saved before Alfred

147

left town. This was not an unusual testimony. This type of scenario was repeated many times.

Having an encounter with the power of God, not only brought people to salvation, it provoked them to service as well. When people were touched by the power of God, they were immediately willing to serve in any way they could to help out.

Psalm 110:3 says: **"Thy people will volunteer freely in the day of Thy power"**(KJV). Because the people in Alfred's meetings had seen and been touched by God's power, they volunteered freely. They wanted to do anything they could to see the revival move forward.

Invariably people would request Alfred and Lillian to stay and pastor the new work, but Alfred would explain that his calling was as an evangelist, not a pastor. But he did help the people organize a church. Many times they organized Sunday schools—which were their church.

Sunday schools at this time were like cell groups or home group meetings today, just larger. They focused on teaching, but also provided an opportunity for relationships and fellowship, giving people a place to receive prayer for personal needs as well.

Beginning a congregation around a Sunday school also did not require that a pastor come and lead the congregation in a traditional way. Instead, it employed the people in teaching and pastoring one another. This released people more quickly in ministry and caused them to mature more quickly.

These Sunday schools generally formed the foundation upon which a "regular" church meeting would be built in the near future. Again, because the people had been touched by the power of God, there was never any lack of teachers or workers for these new churches. This is one reason Alfred could quickly go on to his next assignment.

Remarkably, Alfred not only led large numbers of people to the Lord, but a significant percentage of those saved also received a call into full time ministry. Hundreds of people who met the Lord during these meetings became foreign missionaries as well.

A New Venue

Over the next year, after leaving Bakersfield, Alfred ministered in different cities mostly in southern and central California. But he began having difficulty renting facilities for his meetings. A number of theaters and other venues began refusing to rent to Pentecostals, because they were considered a cult by some of the more traditionally minded.

Alfred did not take no for an answer very well. He was tired of the resistance and difficulty in obtaining places to hold crusades. While vacationing with his family, in between crusades, Alfred decided to fast and pray until God gave him the equipment he needed to hold his crusades. Hannah shares the story.

> *He was so desperate, he said, "we can't get theaters, we can't rent tents, we can't get equipment, and he said…I'm going to pray until God gives me some equipment."*
>
> *We were there on a kind of vacation between meetings, and he started into fasting and praying and he wouldn't undress at night. He'd just put a blanket down, and then he'd lie on the floor.*
>
> *Some nights there wasn't a sound. Some nights there was just a cry; just a groan…and I could hear him all night long. In the mornings, he'd get up, and go and shower, and put on fresh clothes, and go about his activities in the day, but when night would come, I'd say, darling, are you coming to bed tonight?*
>
> *Fasting and praying, 19 days and nights…and at the end of the 19 nights of prayer, he said, I've got the answer, but he didn't have it. He said "God's just…He's going to give it to me." And at the end of the 19 days, a woman came in…she had 160 acres of vineyards, she was a widow woman, never had any children, and servants to work the grounds.*

And she gave him a check for $10,000. We bought a tent, 150 feet long, square, and it was built to order. We bought chairs, a baby grand piano, a beautiful truck that was closed in—all that. She gave him the check for cash to buy it. And he looked at me one day and he smiled. He said, "you know, it pays to fast and pray for 19 nights." That is the only way he ever got anything.

This gift equaled close to $100,000 in today's money. With it Alfred purchased everything he needed to hold crusades in different cities. He also decided to expand his travels further north into Oregon and Washington State.

Fire in the Hole

Alfred was not just persistent when it came to prayer and fasting. He was also persistent when it came to obstacles and difficulties that emerged against his meetings. One good example was his series of meetings in Klamath Falls, Oregon.

Alfred was invited to Klamath Falls by an acquaintance who also offered to help with preparations for the meetings. Understandably then, Alfred expected to have no difficulty finding a venue for their campaign, so they left their truck and tent in California. However, when they arrived in Klamath Falls, no one would rent space to them for their meetings.

This made Alfred even more determined to do the meetings. Soon they found a great place to hold the meetings—a hole in the ground. There was a huge pit available, dug for the foundation of a building that had never been built. Over time people had habitually dumped their trash and refuse there. Alfred thought this hole in the ground would work fine.

Alfred, Hannah, and Alfred, Jr. cleaned up the trash, weeded the grassy areas, and built a platform and benches to seat the people. They also built an overhanging roof covering the last portion of seats, creating an "amphitheater." They advertised the meetings by driving around town in their Cadillac while shouting through a megaphone.

Although people in the city were curious, the first couple of nights Alfred preached to an empty amphitheater. There were people attending, but no one who came would sit on the benches; they were not willing to commit to anything too outrageous. Instead they parked their cars outside the seating area and listened to Alfred preach—from a safe distance.

As this unfolded the first night, Alfred announced he would receive an offering. He told the people if they wanted to contrib-

Alfred, Hannah, and Alfred, Jr.

ute to blink their headlights and he would send someone out to collect their cash. Lights began blinking everywhere.

Over the next few days, as they deemed it safe, people began leaving their cars and came into the pit. Two weeks later, the power fell. Hundreds were saved and many were healed as well. The town embraced the Garrs and their last services were held in the town armory before Alfred and Hannah left to pioneer another work.

Non-Religious Religion

People were often awed by Alfred's ministry. During these years of traveling ministry he became known as *"The man who prays sick people well."* To many people he seemed larger than life, because of his faith and the power demonstrated in his meetings.

Although Alfred was a deeply committed believer, he was not religious. He would fast and pray in a heartbeat for anything he needed.

He took seasons of waiting on God and pursuing Him personally, not just for ministry. But unlike some religious people, he did not focus his life on avoiding fun, but on pursuing God.

In fact, he loved to have fun. Before leaving Oregon, Alfred somehow obtained a black bear cub for his son Alfred, Jr. This bear traveled with them for the next year, as his son's pet. Of course as it grew larger, some people were unnerved by the bear. When Alfred, Jr. moved to Riverside to finish high school, the town required them to give the bear away, which they did—to a zoo.

Early in Alfred's ministry, every vacation was a working vacation. But during the 1920s he became increasingly comfortable taking short breaks and vacations in between campaigns. As his family grew, Alfred began taking more time to spend in recreation with them.

During one particular vacation, Alfred was camping along the Rogue River near Medford Falls, Oregon and fishing. He joined two other men who were also fishing there. One of the men came to Lord shortly after discovering that Alfred was a minister. He then asked Alfred to hold meetings at the local dance hall. Alfred agreed as long as it would not interfere with the fishing.

When the meetings began, the owner of the dance hall gave his life to God and the facility was never used as a dance hall again. People came from all over the surrounding areas for these meetings. A large number of people were saved, healed, and baptized in the Holy Spirit, and the spiritual climate of the area was dramatically changed.

Unemotional Healing Meetings

During the middle to late 1920s, a number of healing evangelists were gaining notoriety, either regionally or nationally. Aimee Semple McPherson, who had stayed at Alfred's missionary home in Hong Kong, had become famous in Los Angeles. Many of these evangelists were quite flamboyant and dramatic in their ministry, and their lives.

Alfred fit this mold of the flamboyant healing evangelist in several ways, but not all of them. He was dramatic in his preaching style and was a very sharp dresser. His wife was beautiful and his son a remarkably handsome, young man. But his healing ministry style was really quite sedate.

Although he was dramatic in his preaching, Alfred took a different approach to praying for the sick. He believed that "jazzing people up" was counterproductive to healing. Instead, soft music would be played and Alfred prayed earnestly, but not boisterously nor with great bombast.

Alfred struggled with how some of the other healing evangelists performed their ministry. In fact, he became somewhat critical of Charles Price, another well-known minister. Although they had never met, Alfred heard about Price's meetings and did not like some of the things that were happening.

Keeping an Open Mind

Charles Price's meetings were wild. As he prayed for people they would often jerk violently around and then were slain in the Spirit, falling down and out. There was also a lot of noise and a lot of what some people considered "show."

One time as Alfred and his driver were going through Portland, Oregon, they saw that Price was holding meetings there. Alfred began complaining to his driver about the extremes in Price's meetings, contrasting it with his own, moderate style of healing services.

As he did this, Alfred immediately got an excruciating headache that would not disappear. The Lord spoke to Alfred to go meet Price and have him pray for him, and he would be healed. Alfred realized the headache had come the moment he began to criticize Charles Price, but he still argued with the Lord until he had driven through the town.

Eventually though, Alfred had his driver turn the car around and head for Price's tent. They arrived just as the afternoon meetings had ended. Alfred approached, introduced himself, and asked Charles Price to pray for him. When he did, Alfred immediately started jerking violently and was slain in the Spirit. He woke up humbled, but healed.

Alfred now realized that God could move how He chose through whomever He chose. But Alfred did not change his own approach; he simply changed his opinion. He continued in his style and recognized that Price simply had a different anointing and spiritual adminis-tration. The two of them became lifelong friends and vacationed together several times.

Keeping the Faith and Zeal

Even though the Garrs enjoyed tremendous success in their ministry, Alfred did not soften in the wrong ways as a result of this success. He and Hannah continued to live a life of aggressive faith. They could have ceased pioneering works and created a comfortable living for themselves at any point, but the thought never really crossed their minds. They were committed to living a sacrificial life which served God and others, not themselves.

The way they chose to handle their finances also revealed the depths of their faith. After a revival campaign ended, they would often keep just enough money to get started in the next location. They would give the rest of the money away to missions. They were committed to trusting God, and financial integrity and a life of giving was central to that.

They also continued trusting God with their health as well. Near the end of 1926 their four-year old daughter, Evangeline, became quite ill. They prayed for her but to no avail, so they contacted a doctor. After examining her, the doctor diagnosed her with diphtheria. This was one of the most common causes of childhood death prior to the introduction of vaccines.

Alfred was also supposed to begin a series of meetings in Angelus Temple, overseeing the congregation there for three months while Aimee Semple McPherson took some time off. The very day he was set to begin these meetings, the doctor had planned to return to the Garr's residence to quarantine "Vangie."

Alfred, Hannah, and Alfred, Jr. prayed for "Vangie," throughout the night asking God to heal and spare her as she screamed deliriously. She began sleeping in the morning. When the doctor arrived to quarantine her, he was shocked. He pronounced her well and forgot any thought of quarantine.

Alfred went to Angelus Temple that day full of faith as a result of Vangie's healing. He continued there for the first three months of 1927, leading the congregation in Aimee's absence. Aimee trusted Alfred enough to lead the congregation because of their long-term friendship. Alfred, Jr. had actually sung publicly for the first time when he was eight years old at the opening of Angelus Temple.

The Other Coast

Over the course of the last five years, Alfred and Hannah had birthed remarkable revivals in Bakersfield, Riverside, Fresno, Long Beach, and San Bernadino, California. They had also found great success in several cities in Oregon and Washington State as well. Plus they visited many smaller towns on their way from these larger campaigns. And they had left new or emerging congregations in each place.

In the spring of 1927, they switched venues and traveled to the East Coast—feeling a burden for that part of the country. They arrived in Norfolk, Virginia and began to pray and look for a meeting location. This was Alfred's first time on the East Coast in a number of years, but the pattern that had begun in Bakersfield started again here.

Finding an empty lot, he set up the tent and began the meetings. He plowed through a couple of weeks of indifference trying to lay a foundation that God would move upon. Soon people began responding to his messages, and to the healing power which emerged. The healings were so powerful the local newspaper carried a big headline.

The Virginian-Pilot

Remarkable Cures Through Prayers
of Preacher Told At Meeting By Those Cured

Persons with Cancer, "Ossified" Bones, Broken Limbs, and Heart Trouble Testify of Miracles Worked by Rev. A.G. Garr and Faith

Much attention had been aroused by the reputed cures being effected through faith and prayer at a tent meeting being conducted at Twenty-fourth and Granby Streets by the Rev. A.G. Garr, an evangelist, who recently conducted a series of services in Angelus Temple, Aimee Semple McPherson's Los Angeles Tabernacle.

The pattern of success the Garrs had found on the West Coast was replicated in the Southeast, as well. After this very successful time in Norfolk, Alfred, and Hannah went on to Miami and Atlanta, and then back up to Virginia Beach holding revival campaigns in each place. The meetings were so powerful in Atlanta that six congregations were birthed as a result.

Accessing the Keys

The keys to Alfred's success in revivals and church planting were prayer, power, persistence, personal hunger, and a pressure free approach to ministry. Through these keys Alfred opened the way for tens of thousands of people to meet the Lord and more than a hundred churches to be birthed in eight remarkable years of ministry.

1) **Prayer** – Alfred's commitment to prayer was legendary. He "prayed through" for direction and provision for meetings. He also prayed through for healing and deliverance for others as well. His aggressive path of faith required him to live and breathe prayer.

2) **Power** – Alfred's success was dependent on spiritual power. He went into difficult areas and unprepared places. If God did not release power, Alfred had no hope. But God always honored his faith by releasing spiritual power.

3) **Persistence** – Alfred was like a pit bull. When he locked down on something he would not let go until it was accomplished. He persisted with God and he persisted in plowing through difficulties, until he received what he had been promised—success.

4) **Personal Hunger** – Alfred's ministry was fresh because he lived out of a fresh experience with God. His desire for God was never satiated by his success nor did it wane through the cares of the world. He maintained his personal hunger for God throughout his life and it kept him from sin and compromise.

5) **Pressure Free** – Alfred only took the burden of the Lord. He never picked up anyone else's burden. Even though there was a natural pressure to stay and pastor the works which emerged from his evangelistic campaigns, Alfred knew he was not responsible for them. He would have dishonored God if he had stayed behind, when God was leading him on. He had a calling to "sow and go." And he did.

He also did not pressure people into quick decisions. He provided an opportunity and was clear about consequences, but would not hurry the process. People were encouraged that God would meet them, if they sought Him. Alfred provided them that opportunity.

The Next Phase

After returning to Los Angeles in the autumn of 1928, for the birth of their second and last daughter, Gloria, Alfred and Hannah were on the move again almost immediately. Within a week after giving birth to Gloria, they were traveling through California visiting some of the churches that were planted from their campaigns.

They continued traveling in California throughout 1929. However, in December they headed back to the East Coast to continue their ministry there. They arrived in Miami, Florida, and stayed there briefly before continuing on to Tampa.

As they were in transit to the East Coast and all during the meetings in Tampa, the Lord kept speaking one word to Alfred repeatedly—"Charlotte." He concluded that the Lord was directing him to Charlotte, North Carolina for his next evangelistic campaign. He could never have imagined what would occur there.

CHAPTER 11

THE FINAL PLANT

Alfred, Hannah, and family arrived in Charlotte, North Carolina in late April of 1930. Charlotte was a small, southern town with a population of around 80,000, whose claim to fame was still to come. Alfred knew no one in Charlotte, but that was not unusual—he often knew no one or almost no one when he came into a new area.

The Garrs were almost out of money when they arrived in Charlotte. They were also, still waiting for their tent to arrive—it had been held up as they passed through the Panama Canal on their way from Los Angeles to the East Coast. Without any contacts in Charlotte, they needed to rent a tent until theirs arrived.

Garr Tent meeting

Alfred spent his time praying and looking for a tent, and a place to put it up. Two weeks after arriving in Charlotte, Alfred located a vacant lot near the city center to pitch the tent, which he was still searching for. Shortly after, a local Baptist church agreed to rent him their tent for two hundred dollars a month. Now with a tent and a location, he and his family were ready to begin their meetings.

Several years earlier, Alfred had obtained a reputation as "The man who prays sick people well." After this reputation developed, he began using this phrase as a slogan to draw the sick and unsaved to his meetings. In Charlotte, they placed a sign over the tent which read, *"Come and hear Evangelist A.G. Garr, the man who prays sick people well. Bring the sick, God will heal them."* Alfred was already laying his reputation on the line and the meetings had not yet begun.

An Inauspicious Beginning

On Mother's Day, May 11, 1930, at three in the afternoon, the meetings began. There were seventeen people in attendance including Alfred, Hannah, Alfred, Jr., Evangeline, and Gloria. Alfred played his trombone, Hannah the piano, and Alfred, Jr. led the singing and worship. Alfred preached but did not receive an offering, considering the crowd was so small.

The evening meeting was better attended since most people were now free from their Mother's Day obligations. There were about seventy-five people in the tent at the Sunday evening meeting. The crowd was polite and things moved slowly, but this was not unusual for the first day or week of meetings in a new city.

Other than an increase in the size of the crowd, little else good happened the rest of that first week. Although Alfred was an interesting speaker, the crowds were still small, and the offerings were smaller. They barely afforded the Garrs enough to buy meals that week, much less to put anything away for the tent rental. But the worst was yet to come. On Friday night, a huge thunderstorm struck and began blowing the tent around violently.

Rainwater filled the tent, so people had to stand on benches just to keep dry while Alfred continued preaching. Alfred, Jr. and some other men worked to keep the tent from toppling over from the wind which was uprooting trees and knocking down fences around them. Hannah took their daughters out to their car, because they were screaming in fear of the lightning. Things were not looking good at the moment.

Demonstration of the Spirit and Power

Alfred and family survived the storm and completed their first week of meetings the next day. It was then that things started to turn around. On Sunday afternoon, one week after the meetings had begun, something dramatic happened. A lady was brought to the tent in critical condition. She had three distinct, serious illnesses—two internal disorders and a problem with her neck. Her neck was swollen larger than her head and was infested internally with maggots. Everyone's attention was drawn to her as she was placed carefully on pillows in the tent.

In the middle of his message, Alfred stopped and looked at this lady, named Mrs. Presley, and declared, "I don't know what her trouble is, but if you will bring her to the platform God will heal her today." With that declaration of faith, Alfred had everyone's attention.

Some men hoisted Mrs. Presley onto the stage and Alfred began to pray for her healing. As he prayed, she jumped up, shouted, and began running up and down the aisles of the tent. She was instantly healed of all three conditions in response to prayer and faith (she passed the maggots several days later). One hundred people witnessed Mrs. Presley's healing at this meeting, but that was not enough for her.

She was so excited about what God had done for her, instead of going home that afternoon and relaxing, Mrs. Presley went throughout town, knocking on doors and telling people about how God had healed her at the tent meetings. That night the tent was filled to overflowing, but this time it was people, not water which flooded the tent.

Wherever Alfred had preached before, the power of God had brought success. People were captivated when the power of God was demonstrated. They flocked to the meetings, bringing their friends, both sick and well when the power fell. But there was something about the way the people of Charlotte responded that was different.

They were so deeply impacted and so grateful, it touched Alfred's heart in a unique way. Charlotte was by no means a wicked city—

there was a substantial church presence there, although a traditional one. But it seemed as if the people of Charlotte had been waiting all their lives for God to move. They had heard about His power, but they had never seen it—at least not like this.

When they saw God's power, the people of Charlotte almost instantly rallied to Alfred. He was different from other ministers because he did not just talk about God's power—he demonstrated it. Instead of seeking answers to why people were sick, Alfred had sought for power to heal their diseases. He believed that *power to change* their situation was better than *answers to explain* their situation.

The Charlotte Observer

Less than two weeks after Alfred began his meetings, the local newspapers began mentioning them because of the healings. Then on June 12, 1930, after only one month, the newspaper published the following headline and article. Once again, the newspapers became heralds of the gospel and God's power to heal.

The Charlotte Observer

Blind, Halt And Lame Testify To Marvelous Cures By Faith

Garr Tent Meeting on West Trade Street Attracts Many Who Claim Recovery From Infirmities.

A woman who said she can now see with an eye that was totally blind, another who is able to walk normally after having an ossified knee joint for many years, a paralyzed Mexican campaign veteran who declared he is gaining the use of himself again, and many other heretofore suffering from various ills and deformities testified last night at the A.G. Garr tent meeting to remarkable faith cures...

One week later on June 18, 1930 another article appeared, outlining additional healings and miracles.

The Charlotte Observer

Miraculous Cures Are Related By Sufferers At Faith Healing

Garr Meeting Here Attracts Crippled Man Who Throws Away Crutches and Walks; Deaf Woman Says She Hears.

Scenes reminiscent of pictures of Biblical times were reenacted last night at the tent on West Trade Street where Dr. A. G. Garr, Los Angeles Evangelist is conducting revival meetings, as more than a score of cripples and sufferers of various ailments after having been prayed over by the preacher, testified to miraculous healing...

The crowds increased again because of the notoriety gained through these articles. People began coming from other parts of North Carolina as well as South Carolina, Georgia, Tennessee, and Virginia because God was healing sick people.

Alfred began feeling that the East Coast was "a neglected field." He was moved with compassion when he saw people coming from such far distances to be taught and healed. He was touched by the Lord's heart for this part of the country, seeing the faith of the people.

A Change of Venue

While Alfred was used to seeing demonstrations of power, the quantity and quality of healings was greater in Charlotte than any other place he had been with the exception of Atlanta. There seemed to be an atmosphere of faith every time they met under the tent. The crowds never diminished, even though most people had to stand around the border of the tent.

After three months of meetings, Alfred felt he had fulfilled his purpose. The power had fallen. Large numbers of people had been saved and healed, so he felt that it was time to move north to Ohio before the winter weather precluded holding meetings there. Alfred announced his plans to depart shortly, but the people had other ideas.

When Alfred made the announcement that he was leaving, the people actually groaned out loud. Alfred had heard objections to his leaving in other cities many times before, but he based his life on the will of God, not the opinion of the people. God did speak to him, however, and surprised Alfred by what He said.

The Lord instructed Alfred to stay and continue through the winter to help establish the people. Alfred quickly made the announcement and the people rejoiced that things would continue. However, Alfred had no desire to simply continue the meetings; he looked to carry them forward and take additional ground. He had little to no ability to maintain—he had to advance.

4,000 seat wooden tabernacle in Charlotte, North Carolina, July/August, 1930

Since the tent had been filled to almost double its seating capacity for quite some time now, Alfred looked for larger facilities to maximize his impact. He purchased the lumber from the Charlotte

Speedway which was being demolished. This was a wooden tongue and groove racetrack, and the lumber was hauled to the lot where the tent stood and was used to construct a wooden tabernacle. When it was completed this tabernacle seated several thousand people.

God Moves With Them

Many times when a revival or series of meetings is moved to another facility, God seemingly does not make the move. There are countless stories of revivals ending because the leaders changed venues to accommodate more people or for the sake of convenience. But that was not the case when Alfred moved their meetings in Charlotte to a new venue.

The first meeting in this wooden tabernacle was filled with excitement as the people felt this facility gave permanence to the revival. In this type of exciting, faith filled atmosphere, a woman was carried into the meeting, wrapped in sheets. She was suffering from a life threatening disease which affected many in the southern United States during the first part of the twentieth century.

Mrs. Rutledge suffered from pellagra. This disease was almost at epidemic stages throughout the South at various times before 1935 and for a while was thought to be contagious like leprosy. Pellagra causes painful skin eruptions and an oozing of blood from the pores. It also eventually produces hallucinations and dementia in advanced stages.

Mrs. Rutledge was carried into the meeting with soft sheets wrapping her body. She was barefoot because her skin was so sensitive and painful that they could not put slippers on her. She was placed on pillows in the tabernacle just as Mrs. Presley had been in the tent. She could not even sit in a chair because of the pain.

When Alfred prayed for her, Mrs. Rutledge stood up and began walking across the platform as the sores on her body began breaking open. Within three days, she was completely healed as no sores remained and her skin was as pink and new as a baby. She returned to the tabernacle within the week to testify to everyone of how God had healed her. God moved in the tabernacle, just as He did in the tent.

This wooden tabernacle became the final resting place for crutches, wheelchairs, and other medical aids discarded when someone was healed. When crippled people were healed, they would often throw their crutches away and these would be suspended from the wooden beams. These devices were left hanging on the beams to testify of the healing power purchased for us when Jesus had hung on wooden beams almost two thousand years earlier.

As the winter months grew colder, the people added walls to the tabernacle so it would retain heat and the meetings could continue in spite of cold weather. Giant oil burning stoves were created to heat the facility, fueled with discarded crankcase oil they reclaimed from service stations and filtered for use as heating oil.

Advancing During the Great Depression

As the meetings continued through the winter months, Alfred began to hear from the Lord that he was supposed to stay long-term. The Lord showed him that he should stay and lead the new congregation. A Sunday school was organized in April 1931 and the congregation was born.

Still not content without making advances, Alfred began looking for permanent facilities. However, securing a building large enough for the current crowd and future expansion would take a miracle. Thankfully, Alfred believed in miracles and had seen a few in his day. But their economic situation was more than grim.

By 1931, the Great Depression had swept America and the rest of the world. Unemployment hovered around 25 percent of the available work force nationally. Borrowing money for a new building was not a possibility—almost five thousand banks across the nation had closed their doors in the previous two years. So Alfred did the only thing he could to obtain the building—he fasted and prayed.

While fasting and praying about a facility, Alfred saw a notice that the Charlotte Civic Auditorium was up for sale. Alfred soon received a word from God that astounded everyone around him— God was going to give them the auditorium for their building.

So Alfred visited the auditorium the Lord had promised him and enquired about the price. He was told that the bare minimum the city would accept for the auditorium was $225,000. They might as well have asked for the moon. The congregation had no money and no chance of obtaining any significant funds from any source. Still Alfred thanked God in faith for giving them the building, and turned and walked away.

Two weeks later, the rug was pulled out from under them. Alfred was driving through town and saw the Civic Auditorium being torn down. Shocked, Alfred ran into the building and discovered that the new owners were only interested in the land. Alfred asked what they would sell the building for. They offered to sell him the bricks, lumber, and steel beams for $2500. Alfred agreed on the spot—even though he still had no money.

Kingdom Finances

That night Alfred announced to the congregation that he had purchased the City Auditorium for one percent of the original asking price. The people gasped in excitement and disbelief. They were excited they had gotten their building, but in disbelief because they had no money to pay for it. The congregation gave sacrificially in an offering that evening and Alfred collected the $2500 needed to pay for the materials.

The next week a couple in the congregation was awakened by the Lord in the middle of night and instructed to make the $2000 down payment on a piece of land for their new building. They did it the next day. Soon trucks were unloading their new building piece by piece onto their new church property.

Alfred had been trusting God for finances since his Burning Bush days. He claimed to not have been tempted to doubt God since 1906 on the point of financial provision—not since his encounter with God on the ship going to India. But now Alfred was required to believe God for the finances for a congregation and a building program, not just his family.

The list of financial responsibilities was imposing. They had daily expenses for the truck drivers who were delivering their building. Alfred was responsible for paying the skilled masons, carpenters, and other workers who would rebuild the auditorium on their property. But God came through in every case.

Sometimes God would speak to a person in the congregation to give a certain amount of money. At other times a letter would arrive from someone who had been healed in one of Alfred's campaigns in another state and would include a check. Many times Alfred simply sacrificed personally, as he had done countless times before, to see the workers paid.

Alfred had been swimming against the stream his entire ministry. Now he did it on another level. When businesses and individuals were retreating during the Great Depression, Alfred was advancing. When companies were cutting jobs, Alfred was providing them. When it seemed that everyone was circling the wagons, Alfred was charging the enemy.

The congregation volunteered their time freely. Every evening people would come to the property and clean mortar off the bricks that the masons would use the next day. It was not unusual for people to spend their evenings talking, singing, or praying and cleaning brick. It was a congregational team building time.

Alfred agreed to pay a daily wage of $1 plus lunch for each of the workers. This was a good deal for those who had been out of work due to the Depression. The ladies of the church would come daily and prepare lunch for the workers. Alfred never missed a single payment to any worker or any company during the construction of their facility.

Remarkably, the work went smoothly, until it came time to erect the steel beams. Then there was a brief panic. No one could locate the plans for the steel beams, because the auditorium had been built twenty-six years previously. The city could not find the plans—they had been lost some years back. Finally after much anxious prayer, the plans were located and the building resumed.

The Garr Auditorium in Charlotte, North Carolina

On June 18, 1933 after two years of construction, Alfred led the congregation in a victory march. The entire congregation walked the short distance from the wooden tabernacle they had occupied for over two years to their new permanent facility, which was named Garr Auditorium. They moved in debt free during the Depression, which was miraculous. The facility was not completely finished on the inside, but was ready to be occupied.

Be Fruitful

Although Alfred was now pastoring a single congregation instead of traveling and establishing congregations, his approach remained much the same. Although the name of their facility was the Garr Auditorium, the name of the congregation was the Carolina Evangelistic Association.

Although a strange name for a church, it revealed Alfred's focus and approach as a pastor. His goal with the Carolina Evangelistic Association was to train, equip, and release believers to do the work of the ministry. He was not interested in being a traditional pastor who simply threw some food to the sheep every week. He believed God could raise up other believers without a spiritual pedigree—like himself—who could change their world with the gospel and faith.

Alfred believed the church was supposed to be a gathering and training place, not a retirement home. He believed that people would attend the Carolina Evangelistic Association for a few years of training and equipping in the gospel of ministry and faith, and then they could be released into mission work, either in church planting in the United States or as foreign missionaries. He believed that every Christian could be used by God in both power and demonstration of the Spirit—they just needed role models, some training, and opportunities to minister.

For the next decade, through the Carolina Evangelistic Association, Alfred trained, equipped, and released hundreds of missionaries and ministers into their calling and ministries. A number of churches were planted in other parts of the South and in several other countries.

The Charlotte congregation also quickly became the leading Pentecostal Church on the East Coast. It continued as a regional resource center for churches, ministries, and individuals on the eastern seaboard and throughout the South for the next fifty years.

... And Multiply

As an evangelist, Alfred had faithfully sowed seeds of the gospel throughout America and the nations for the first thirty-three years of the twentieth century. But now God had another plan for him. Instead of Alfred simply sowing the seeds, the Lord planted him as a seed into the people of Charlotte, North Carolina. The fruit that emerged was remarkable.

In addition to hundreds of missionaries and ministers who were trained and had emerged from the Carolina Evangelistic Association, Alfred's family began emerging into their own gifts and callings during this time as well.

Hannah had been teaching and providing leadership in many of their campaigns for years. She often taught the people when they held afternoon meetings. In Charlotte, she functioned as a pastor along with Alfred. He traveled in ministry periodically after the permanent facility was completed, and Hannah led the congregation in his absence—often for months at a time.

In 1937, she launched a radio-teaching ministry which continued for more than forty years throughout the South. She became a leading figure in the Pentecostal movement in the United States through her teaching ministry and the influence of the Carolina Evangelistic Association.

Alfred, Jr. also became remarkably successful. After several years as a sought after singer in Hollywood (he and Bing Crosby were the two most popular tenors during that time), and meritorious service in World War II as a colonel, Alfred, Jr. traveled in missions work in Germany, India, and other nations.

He also established a summer camp for children and teenagers known as Camp Lurecrest in North Carolina, an outreach of the church which continues to this day. Additionally, he pioneered Christian television and films with Willard Cantelon, a noted Christian author and missionary.

Evangeline, or Vangie, continued to serve for years as a leader in the training programs of the Carolina Evangelistic Association and as a teacher among the youth and children. Subsequently, she also assisted her brother in pioneering Camp Lurecrest.

After Gloria married, she and her husband, Bob McAllister, traveled to Brazil to serve as missionaries assisting Lester Sumerall. They moved to Brazil permanently several years later to pioneer a church. The Lord blessed their efforts, and they eventually established and were responsible for overseeing two hundred congregations in Brazil, Portugal, and South Africa.

The testimonies of the life of Alfred Garr, his family, and those he impacted could fill other books. Dr. Alfred Goodrich Garr graduated from this life to eternity on July 23, 1944. He went to be with the Lord on his seventieth birthday. His life was full, his influence was wide, and the impact of his life was deep. He was a hero of the faith and a true apostle in the twentieth century.

A Prophetic Sign

Alfred was never limited by tradition throughout his life and ministry. He followed God and got results because he attempted things that others thought were impossible, or too different from the norm. Although this was one of the key sources of his success in ministry, it also brought about much misunderstanding and persecution.

Some of the misunderstandings and persecution were the standard fare that pioneers have to endure, but one rumor in Charlotte was especially strange. In spite of the high financial integrity and faith which Hannah and Alfred demonstrated, someone started the ludicrous rumor that upon his death, his family planned to sell the auditorium, take the money, and skip town.

Although this rumor was totally unfounded, Alfred did something about it. Before his death, he gave instructions that his body should be interred in the church facility. He reasoned that if his body were buried there it would give assurance to the community that his family would not sell the church property and abscond with the money.

So after his death, his family complied with Alfred's desire. A small crypt was prepared and his body was interred in an alcove which was a part of the foundation of the church building. Alfred

Garr was planted in the church which he had sacrificially built and faithfully served.

This is not just an interesting part of Alfred's story—it is also a prophetic sign. Alfred Garr's bones became part of the foundation of a church that walked in amazing power, spiritual authority, and influence. His bones were planted there as an assurance that the church would not abandon its spiritual calling and sell out to the temporal things of this world.

This is the purpose of Alfred Garr's life story being revealed now. If we can touch his bones—the core values of his life—we can be revived and stand to our feet. If we will adopt his passion, his faith, and his sacrificial commitment to God, we can find the same power and spiritual authority he found.

And if these bones become planted in the foundation of the church in our generation, we too can avoid the temptation of choosing the temporal over the spiritual. By planting these core values in the foundation of our lives, ministries, and congregations, we can overcome any Laodicean lukewarmness, and faithfully and zealously love and serve God in our generation.

Touch the bones of Alfred Garr. Let the power of these core values reawaken your zeal, your love, and your faith in God. May we find the same endurance to never give up and never give in. And may we find the same hunger for God that can never be quenched.

CORE VALUES—THE BONES OF ALFRED GARR

1) Spiritual Hunger

Alfred was continually hungry for God. He never allowed his spiritual hunger to wane through any hardship, disappointment, or success that he experienced. He was a lifelong lover of God.

Many believers tend to lose their heart and hunger for God either through the cares of this world, the deceitfulness of riches, or the lust of other things which enter in (see Mark 4:19). But Alfred was able to overcome all of these and to cultivate increasing spiritual hunger throughout his life.

Even after attaining acclaim and prominence, Alfred remained more focused on the Lord than on his success. One reason was that he chose to build his life around pleasing God, not establishing a reputation for himself. This kept his heart from drifting away from the Lord, as he became increasingly successful and famous.

Alfred was also a lifelong student. He never felt that he had attained, but he continually sought more in God. He was also a man of the Word. These spiritual disciplines kept the spiritual fire inside of him burning throughout his life.

2) Just Do Something—Now

Alfred was a man who moved quickly. He was not driven by pressure—he was *launched* through faith. He believed that God would move in response to his faith, so he continually gave God something to bless by attempting to do what others probably would not have done.

Alfred also believed that anything worth doing was worth doing now. Whenever he saw God's will or received specific direction from Him, he moved out quickly.

Another reason he moved quickly was because he understood the brevity of life. The loss of his first two daughters on the mission field and his first wife in the United States emphasized this truth to him. Alfred realized that none of us are promised another day, so he made every day count for the kingdom of God.

3) Do not Despise Your Past

After being baptized in the Holy Spirit in 1906, Alfred could have easily despised his past and his mistakes in the Burning Bush movement. But God had used this group to train, equip, and prepare him for the next forty years of his life and ministry, and Alfred realized that.

Although he repudiated the wrong practices the Burning Bush had fallen into, Alfred never lost sight of the good they had given him or the good they had done through their ministry.

Alfred was trained in faith, sacrificial living, a practical approach to ministry, and devotion to the Scriptures in the Burning Bush. He probably would not have been successful on the foreign fields, or at home, without this training and the opportunities the Burning Bush had provided him.

4) Prayer and Fasting

Alfred was a man of prayer and fasting. He prayed for direction; he prayed for provision; he prayed for physical healing for sick people. He found a place of power and authority with God through his devotion to prayer.

Hannah said that prayer and fasting was the only way Alfred ever got anything. When confronted with insurmountable obstacles, Alfred prayed and fasted. Twice that we know of, he fasted and prayed for weeks at a time, and God released miraculous provision for the church and himself in response. Alfred saw amazing results because he was willing to pay the price through prayer and fasting.

5) The Necessity of Power

Alfred was dependent on the power of God. If he had chosen a more traditional ministry, he might have been able to get by with his preaching gift, because he was a wonderful speaker. But Alfred was called to an apostolic life and ministry. Because he was pioneering churches, like Paul, he needed demonstrations of the Spirit and power to confirm the gospel, not just nice sermons based on human wisdom.

Alfred often had to endure some difficult meetings as he waited on God to move in power. He would begin his campaigns by preaching and teaching until the people repented and their faith in God was built up. But when the people began turning to God, the Lord began releasing healing power in response. As a result of his dependence on God's power, he found remarkable success in winning souls.

6) Staying in Your Calling

Alfred seldom strayed from his calling. When the Lord called him to travel as an evangelist, Alfred continued in it despite the sacrifices it required. He never sought the comfort or security of a pastorate. If he had abandoned his calling for security or prominence, many people would have been untouched by the Lord. Although he was asked repeatedly to pastor the congregations which emerged from his evangelistic campaigns, Alfred stayed his course and fulfilled his calling to pioneer.

He not only succeeded in his calling, but as a result, he helped others find success in their callings as well. Whenever Alfred held evangelistic campaigns, a congregation would be established. In some cases as many as six congregations were established through one campaign. Consequently, many others were released into pastoral ministry because Alfred would not step out of his role as an evangelist to fill theirs as pastors.

7) Kingdom Finances

Alfred operated his ministry with high financial integrity, but even more so with faith. When traveling as an evangelist, he would often fast and pray in the money needed for campaigns and equipment. But he seldom kept any money for very long. He usually gave away whatever he had to missions or others who were beginning in ministry.

For example, during the 1920s, he discipled his personal driver in faith and ministry principles, and eventually gave him a tent so he could launch out into evangelistic ministry. James James, his former driver, used this tent and the lessons he learned from Alfred to hold evangelistic campaigns which established twenty-five churches.

For as long as he or Hannah pastored the congregation, the church continued functioning in amazing faith. After paying the bills for the congregation each month, they gave away what was left over to support missionaries or other ministers. They stayed in a place of depending on the Lord for finances and God honored their faith.

8) Judge Nothing Before the Time

This was a profound key to Alfred's success and poses an interesting question for us. When was Alfred Garr most successful? Was it in India, Hong Kong, or Japan? Was it when he pastored The Garage in Los Angeles, on the road in the 1920s, or in Charlotte in the 1930s?

Many people would believe Alfred was most successful in Charlotte because that is where he came into greatest prominence. But prominence does not equal success in the kingdom of God. Ultimately, we will not be able to accurately judge Alfred's greatest success until the Lord comes and judges everything. Paul wrote about this principle to the Corinthian church.

Moreover it is required in stewards, that a man be found faithful.

But with me it is a very small thing that I should be judged of you, or of man's judgment: yea, I judge not mine own self.

For I know nothing by myself; yet am I not hereby justified: but he that judgeth me is the Lord.

Therefore judge nothing before the time, until the Lord come, who both will bring to light the hidden things of darkness, and will make manifest the counsels of the hearts: and then shall every man have praise of God (I Corinthians 4:2-5).

Today, we have been trained to continually judge our own success and the successes of others, by the immediate results we see outwardly, but this is foolish. Alfred Garr and other pioneers continue to bear fruit through ventures which they or others may have considered failures when looking at the immediate results. God's perspective is profoundly different than our own—we almost never see things as He does.

This is one reason we must live close to God and walk in obedience. Only by obeying Him can we find real success. Our ability to determine our best path through human assessments of success will almost always be short sighted and may lead us a different way than the Lord would have us go. Our calling is to obey God and judge nothing before the time.

9) People Make the Times

Alfred Garr lived an amazing life. He became a hero of the faith and a true apostle of the twentieth century. But Alfred was not born special—he became special through the grace of God as these core values developed in his life. These bones are available for us to touch and adopt as our own.

Alfred was an ordinary man, who was used by God extraordinarily, because he dared to have faith. God is no respecter of persons, but He is a respecter of faith. He moves in response to faith. Alfred's life is an encouragement for every one of us to press in closer to God and take Him at His Word. We can experience similar results, if we are willing to pay the price Alfred paid.

While discussing Alfred Garr's life and ministry, someone made this statement—"Those were special times—God was just doing a special thing back then." I immediately took exception to the statement and still do, because the underlying sentiment, although well intentioned, is a dangerous course of thought.

Those times were special—there is no doubt about that. However, it was not that God chose to do something, which propelled Alfred and others to walk in remarkable faith and power. If this were true then we would have to wait until God arbitrarily decided to move this way again. But we do not have to wait.

God desires to move this way in every generation. Those times were special, but they were made special by the amazing faith and radical obedience of Alfred Garr and others. The kingdom of God came in response to their faith and obedience—they realized that God was willing and waiting to move on their behalf, and they acted on it.

These are the bones of Alfred Garr's life. Touch them and be revived. Touch them and stand to your feet. We must stop waiting for the times to change. The times are waiting for us to change them. There is no limitation to what we can accomplish in God, if only we will follow Him in faith.

APPENDIX B

LIFE AND TIMES OF ALFRED GARR

November 12, 1853 .... Oliver and Josephine Garr are married.

July 23, 1874 .... Alfred Gaeleton Garr born in Danville, Virginia.

November 4, 1878 ...... Lillian Anderson is born.

1881 .... Alfred begins to seek after God.

September 11, 1888 .... Oliver Garr, Alfred's father, dies.

1889 .... Alfred finds assurance of salvation.

1897 .... Alfred recommits his life to Christ.

September 1898 .... Alfred enrolls in Asbury College.

March 12, 1899 .... Alfred marries Lillian Anderson.

December 1901 .... Alfred and Lillian join the Burning Bush movement.

February 12, 1904 .... Danville, Virginia congregation established.

May 1905 .... Alfred and Lillian's first daughter, Virginia, is born.

February 1906 .... Alfred and family arrive in Los Angeles, California.

June 14, 1906 .... Lillian is baptized in the Holy Spirit.

June 16, 1906 .... Alfred is baptized in the Holy Spirit.

June 21, 1906 .... The Garrs removed from leadership of the Burning Bush.

Mid-late December
1906 .... Alfred and Lillian arrive in Calcutta, India.

July 26, 1907 .... Josephine Garr, Alfred's mother, dies.

October 8, 1907 .... Alfred and Lillian arrive in Hong Kong.

January 1908 .... The Garrs' second daughter, Josephine, dies at birth.

March 20, 1908 .... The Garrs' co-worker, Maria Gardner, dies of smallpox.

March 21, 1908 .... Virginia Garr dies of Small Pox in Hong Kong.

April 1908 .... Alfred and Lillian leave Hong Kong for Japan.

June 1908 .... Alfred and Lillian leave Japan for United States.

July 1908-
September 1909 .... The Garrs travel extensively in North America.

October 4, 1909 .... Alfred and Lillian arrive in Hong Kong.

January 22, 1910 .... Alfred and Lillian leave Hong Kong for India.

November 1910 .... The Garrs return to Hong Kong from India.

April 9, 1911 .... Alfred Gaeleton Garr, Jr. is born in Hong Kong.

January 1912 .... The Garrs arrive in Los Angeles.

1912 – 1913 .... Alfred travels to Arabia and India.

1914 .... Alfred changes his and his son's middle name to Goodrich.

1914 - April 1916 .... Alfred and Lillian pastor The Garage in Los Angeles.

1915 - 1916 .... Alfred serves as Executive Presbyter of Assemblies of God.

April 12, 1916 .... Lillian Garr goes to be with the Lord.

June 1916 .... Alfred healed of stomach cancer.

July 26, 1918 .... Alfred marries Hannah Erickson.

Summer 1919 .... Alfred holds meetings at Lyceum Theater in Los Angeles.

June 1921 .... Alfred healed while preaching in Fresno, California.

August -
September 1922 .... Alfred holds Bakersfield California meetings.

September 12, 1922 .... Evangeline Garr born in Bakersfield, California.

January 1923 .... Angelus Temple opens—Alfred, Jr. sings first solo.

1921 - 1930 .... Alfred establishes over one hundred churches.

October 1928 .... Alfred receives honorary doctorate—Foursquare Church.

October 10, 1928 .... Gloria Garr born in Los Angeles, California.

May 11, 1930 .... Tent meetings begin in Charlotte, North Carolina.

July 26, 1930 .... Meetings move into 4,000 seat wooden tabernacle.

June 18, 1933 .... Congregation moves into permanent facilities.

July 23, 1944 .... Dr. Alfred Goodrich Garr goes to be with the Lord.

BIBLIOGRAPHY

Books

Anderson, Gerald, *Biographical Dictionary of Christian Missions*,
New York, Simon & Schuster Macmillan, 1998.

Anderson, Robert, *Vision of the Disinherited*,
The Making of American Pentecostalism, Peabody,
Hendrickson Publishers, Inc., 1992.

Atter, Gordon, *The Third Force*, Peterborough, Ontario,
The College Press, 1962.

Baker, Isabelle, *Stone Church 50th Anniversary Commemorative Book*,
Yakima, Wa., 1978.

Bartleman, Frank, *Azusa Street*, Plainfield,
Logos International, 1980.

Blumhofer, Edith, *Aimee Semple McPherson: Everybody's Sister*,
Grand Rapids, Mi., Wm. B. Eerdmans Publishing Co., 1993.

Blumhofer, Edith, *The Assemblies of God Vol.1*, Springfield, Mo.,
Gospel Publishing House, 1989.

Burgess, Stanley M.; McGee, Gary B., Alexander, P, *Dictionary of
Pentecostal and Charismatic Movements*, Grand Rapids, Mi.,
Zondervan Publishing House, 1988.

Campbell, Joseph E, *The Pentecostal Holiness Church*, Raleigh,
World Outlook Publications, 1951.

Ewart, Frank J., *The Phenomenon of Pentecost*, Hazelwood, Mo.,
World Aflame Press, 1947.

Ewart, Frank; Kidson W.E., *The Phenomenon of Pentecost*, Houston,
The Herald Publishing House, 1947.

Frodsham, Stanley Howard, *With Signs Following*,
    Springfield, Mo., Gospel Publishing House, 1948.

Garr Auditorium—Eleventh Anniversary, Charlotte, 1941.

Garr, Alfred, *Gems From The Pulpit*, 1927.

King, Joseph H., *Yet Speaketh*, Franklin Springs, Ga.,
    The Publishing House, 1949.

Kostlevy, William, *Nor Silver, Nor Gold: The Burning Bush Movement
    and the Communitarian Holiness Vision*, Dissertation Abstract.

Kulbeck, Gloria G., *What God Hath Wrought*, Toronto,
    The Pentecostal Assemblies of Canada, 1958.

Lang, G, *The Early Years of the Tongues Movement*, circa 1950.

Law, E. May, *Pentecostal Mission Work in South China*, Falcon, N.C.,
    The Falcon Publishing Co., circa late 1915.

Lawrence, B.F., *The Apostolic Faith Restored*, St. Louis, 1916.

Maude Aimee Humbard, *Maude Aimee...I Look to the Hills*, Akron,
    Rex Humbard Ministry, 1976.

McClung, Jr., L. Grant - Ketcham & Warner, *Azusa Street and
    Beyond*, South Plainfield, N.J., Bridge Publishing, Inc, 1986.

McGee, Gary, *The Gospel-shall Be Preached*, Springfield, Mo.,
    The Gospel Publishing House, 1986.

Miller, Thomas William, *Canadian Pentecostals: A History of the
    Pentecostal Assemblies of Canada*.

Mission Community Church 50th Anniversary Edition, Riverside, Ca., 1975.

Mitchell, Robert Bryant, *Heritage & Horizons: The History of the OBSC*,
    Des Miones, Open Bible Publishers, 1982.

Morrris, Eddie, *The Vine and Branches John 15:5*, (By the Author), 1981.

Nichol, John Thomas, *Pentecostalism*, New York, Harper & Row, 1966.

Pentecostal Tabernacle Hong Kong 50th Anniversary, Hong Kong, 1957.

Stanley, Susie Cunningham, *Feminist Pillar of Fire:*
  The life of Alma White, Cleveland, The Pilgrim Press, 1993.

Synan, Vinson, *The Holiness-Pentecostal Movement in the United States*,
  Grand Rapids, Mi., William B. Eerdmans Publishing Co., 1971.

Twentieth Anniversary of the Garr Auditorium, Charlotte, 1950.

Tyson, James L., *The Early Pentecostal Revival*, Hazelwood, Mo.,
  Work Aflame Press, 1992.

Valdez, A.C. Sr., *Fire On Azusa Street*, Costa Mesa, Ca.,
  Gift Publications, 1980.

Vanzandt, J.C., *Speaking in Tongues*, Portland, Or., 1926.

White, Alma, *The Story of My Life & the Pillar of Fire*, Zarephath, N.J.,
  1928.

Woodsworth-Etter, Maria, *Signs & Wonders*, 1918.

NEWSPAPERS
Coulton Courier
Kewanee Star Courier
Los Angeles Examiner
Los Angeles Times
Tampa Tribune
The Atlanta Constitution
The Bakersfield Californian
The Charlotte News
The Charlotte Observer
The Daily Record, Columbia, South Carolina
The Klamath Falls Daily News

The Klamath Falls Evening News
The Miami Daily News
The Miami Herald
The Virginia Pilot
The Yakima Morning Herald

Periodicals
Moorhead, Max Wood, *Cloud of Witnesses To Pentecost in India,*
Bombay, India, 3/1/1908

Pentecostal Power, Calcutta India
The Apostolic Faith, Los Angeles, Californina
The Bride Grooms Messenger, Atlanta, Georgia
The Burning Bush, Chicago, Illinois, Waukesha, Wisconsin 1902—1908
The Christian Evangel, Chicago, Illinois
The Free Methodist, Chicago, Illinois
The Good Report, Los Angeles
The Independent, Boston, Massachusetts
The Later Rain Evangel, Chicago, Illinois
The Moody Church News
The Morning Thought For the Day, Charlotte, North Carolina
The New Acts, Alliance, Ohio
The Pentecostal Evangel, St. Louis/Springfield, Missouri
The Upper Room, Los Angeles, California
The Victorious Gospel, Los Angeles, California
The Word & Witness, Malvern, Alaska
The Word & Works
Treasures, Tulsa, Oklahoma

Other Works

Downing, Rose Pittman, *God Works in Mysterious Ways His Wonders to Perform,* unpublished manuscript.

Fritsch, Homer and Alice, *Letters from Cora,* 1987.

Letters from Blanche Appleby, Rose Pitman, A.G. Garr, Sr

Interviews conducted by Ken Kandel in 1979 of Alfred Garr, Jr., Hannah Garr, the staff and members of Garr Memorial Church.

Interviews conducted by Ken Kandel in 1979 of Gene Robinson, Jimmy Sustar, Willard Cantelon, and the Ketchel Clanton.

Interviews conducted by Steve Thompson in 1995 with Alfred Garr, Jr., Gloria McAllister, and Vangie Garr Beam.

Phone interviews conducted by Adam Gordon with various participants of the revivals in the twenties.

Interview with William Kostlevy in 1997.

McGee, Gary (http://www.agts.edu/faculty/faculty_publications/lectures/mcgee_lecture_sept02.pdf) *The Caluctta Revival of 1907 and The Reformulation of Charles F. Parham's Bible Evidence Doctrine,* published September 2002

General Council of the Assemblies of God 1914 to 1916

Missouri Annual Conference of the MEC South 1908 to 1913

Note: For questions on references or historical information contact Adam Gordon at Garrhistory@aol.com.